THE POLITICAL PHILOSOPHY OF
MARTIN LUTHER KING, JR.

CONTRIBUTIONS IN AFRO-AMERICAN
AND AFRICAN STUDIES

The Political Philosophy of Martin Luther King, Jr.

HANES WALTON, JR.

Introduction by
SAMUEL DuBOIS COOK

CONTRIBUTIONS IN AFRO-AMERICAN
AND AFRICAN STUDIES, NUMBER 10

GREENWOOD PRESS
New York • Westport, Connecticut • London

Walton, Hanes, 1941–
    The political philosophy of Martin Luther King, Jr.
Introd. by Samuel DuBois Cook. Westport, Conn., Greenwood Pub. Corp. [1971]

    xxxviii, 137 p. 22 cm. (Contributions in Afro-American and
African studies, no. 10)

    "A Negro Universities Press publication."
    A revision of the author's thesis, Howard University, 1967.
    Bibliography: p. 119-128.

    1. King, Martin Luther.   I. Title.   (Series)
E185.97.K5W27   320'.01'0924   76-11260
ISBN 0-8371-4661-5   MARC

Library of Congress   71 [4]

Copyright © 1971 by Hanes Walton, Jr.

Library of Congress Catalog Card Number: 76-111260
ISBN: 0-8371-4661-5

First published in 1971, a Negro Universities Press publication

Greenwood Press, Inc.
88 Post Road West, Westport, Connecticut 06881

Printed in the United States of America

The paper used in this book complies with the
Permanent Paper Standard issued by the National
Information Standards Organization (Z39.48-1984).

10 9 8 7

323.4092
K53 Wa

To Professor Emmett E. Dorsey,
Who Has an Abiding Faith
in the Future of America

Contents

Preface

BIOGRAPHIES and autobiographies of black leaders are fairly numerous, but all too few are those studies offering a systematic examination of their intellectual contributions as such. Yet, regardless of the point of view from which the life of any black leader is seen, one theme can be found in common to them all: the quest for freedom, equality, and manhood, that has existed since the black man's arrival on American soil. While it is most commonly presumed that a prerequisite to the attainment of this goal is full and equal integration of blacks and whites, some black leaders have strongly disagreed with either the possibility or the desirability of integration between the black and white races. In the passion of debate between the advocates of black separatism and back-to-Africa movements, and those seeking ever new ways for bringing about the full equality of black people within a dominant white society, little attention has been given the social, economic, and political ideas of black leaders, as philosophies in their own right. Nor have these philosophies been subjected to the thorough analysis and critical assessment they deserve as genuine, frequently original contributions to the mainstream of Western thought.

This book is an inquiry into the political philosophy of one black leader, Martin Luther King, Jr., whose influence on both white and black people, individually and collectively, has been, and continues to be beyond measure. The impact of his personality, leadership, and ideas are of a magnitude and a kind that warrant special consideration of his thought, particularly in relation to what he considered to be the good life and what was implied in the achievement of that dream by nonviolent means. Speaking and acting with striking moral force, King stirred the citizens and the government of the United States from a state of passive indifference toward a problem at the very core of the American psyche, to an attitude of conscious concern and meaningful commitment.

This study will attempt to identify and evaluate the special character and development of King's political philosophy, the problems with which he was primarily concerned, the historical context that nourished his thought, his proposals for social action, and his normative doctrines.

It is hoped that the methodological framework for structuring and organizing King's political philosophy which appears in Chapter Three will be found useful to other students of black political thought in their inquiries.

H. WALTON, JR.

Thunderbolt, Ga.
November, 1969

Acknowledgments

THIS BOOK, originally conceived as a doctoral dissertation at Howard University, owes much to my teachers there, their knowledge of political philosophy in general and black politics in particular. I would especially like to thank Dean C. L. Miller and Professors Emmett E. Dorsey, Harold Gosnell, Nathaniel Tillman, and Morris Levitt for their guidance and their patience.

I would also like to thank Professor Samuel Cook of Duke University for his analysis and advice which both guided and restrained me. Thanks are also owing to my colleagues Professors Brenda Mobley and Thomas Byers for their encouragement and comments. Also, for their constant encouragement I am grateful to Mrs. Lucille Smith, Mr. and Mrs. Arthur Foster, my parents, Mr. and Mrs. Thomas Walton, Mr. and Mrs. Emmett Travis, Margaret Guest, and Gloria Walton.

And, finally, for their indispensable help in typing the manuscript I am most grateful to Estelle Greenfield, Barbara J. Mobley, Lillie Key, and Delores Drummond.

Introduction

The American Liberal Democratic Tradition, the Black Revolution, and Martin Luther King, Jr.

THE BLACK man, since the early days of the fledgling New World, has been a profound and endless embarrassment to American political thought, institutions, and processes. And 'they, in turn, have constituted a deep and infinite offense to the content, form, and aspirations of the black experience. Deep are the wounds of blacks, and vast are the pretensions, concealments, ambiguities, and agonies of American political thought and experience. The tears and fears, hopes and doubts, have rippled and flowed both ways.

Racism is an affliction of the human spirit and an enormous and sad affront to, and burden on, the democratic enterprise. Rival systems of government can make peace with the philosophy of racism but democracy— never. For democracy builds on what unites men, not what separates them; the similarities of men, not their differences, count in the calculus of the democratic way. The only human reality relevant to the democratic organization of power and distribution of rights and privileges, burdens and responsibilities is man qua man, with all his strengths, infirmities, and possibilities. Democratic theory proceeds from the commanding assumption that government is a function of the consent of the governed; that government is the servant—not the master—of the whole body of citizens.

Equality is a cornerstone of the democratic edifice—equality of consideration, participation, opportunity, and legal protection. Equality of citizenship and humanity is the lodestar of democracy. This means, among other things, that power in a democracy is shared by all members of the political community. Monopolistic or disproportionate power by a particular group is as alien to the spirit and substance of democracy as it is essential to alternative structures and processes of government. In a democracy, the ground on which men stand is level. The needs of each individual are weighed equally on the same scales of consideration and decision.

Political philosophers and social theorists as well as theologians and moralists have said a great deal about original sin. Racism is the original sin of the American political system and social order—the Achilles' heel of democratic ideals and achievements. For Negroes have been excluded not only from the realization but from the very *pursuit* of happiness and the *promise* of America.

The contradiction between racism and the country's democratic ideals and commitments has been radical, pervasive, and pathetic; the consequences have been tragic and far-reaching. Moral, spiritual, ideological, and institutional pollution has seeped into and poisoned the bloodstream and environment of the liberal democratic tradition. It has polluted the experiment in self-government, equality, and freedom. The pain and pathos of alienation at the most fundamental level of political conception have been cumulative, simmering beneath the surface. Because of the shameful neglect of the past, they constitute a destructive augury for the future.

For black men, democratic ideals—including the achievements of, and performances for whites—have been a mixed blessing. They are a source of hope and despair, faith and doubt, identity and alienation, inspiration and frustration, comfort and anguish, affection and bitterness, optimism and pessimism, delight and anger. Just as ambivalence and ambiguity have characterized the larger American experience and thought in the context of racism, they have also typified the inner life and structure of meaning of black people. Both black men and white men have wrestled with profound contradictions and ambiguities and have sought desperately to transcend them.

In the drama of American political thought and practice, and in their various complex relationships, black men have been a source of tension, contradiction, and moral rebuke. Their involvement has been enormous and inescapable. Racism is a perpetual embarrassment to democratic idealism and humanism. Various strands of American political thought have spent themselves justifying, analyzing, ignoring, and modifying the oppressive status of Afro-American existence. The task has been neither simple and easy nor entirely successful.

Consider for example, the political thought of the slave controversy from Colonial times to the Declaration of Independence, the Constitutional Convention, and the traumatic intensification and polarization of the 1830s, 1840s, and 1850s until the Civil War and Reconstruction. Apart from the political theory at the time of the Revolution and Constitution, the most productive focus of American political thought has centered on black men—the eloquent attacks on, and fierce defenses of, the "peculiar institution." And one should not forget either the role of slaves as an object of thought in the former, or the brevity of that period of theorizing in comparison with the booming era after 1820. Perhaps the crowning irony of American political thought is that many consider John C. Calhoun, that great and powerful apologist for slavery (apology was the main motivation and keystone of his theoretical edifice), the most "original" and "profound" political theorist this country has produced.

Consider the governing presuppositions and principles of Southern political thought. As a body of propositions, intuitive judgments, and sentiments (or "prejudices," to borrow Fitzhugh's term), Southern political philosophy—as a distinctive system of values—whatever its associations with feudalism, aristocracy, states' rights, agrarianism, sentimental regionalism, and romantic nationalism, is dominated and tyrannized by racism in the form of slavery; its legacy is caste, segregation, and discrimination. Against the mainstream of the American "liberal tradition," Southern political thought, because of the tyranny of racism, has emphasized inequality, privilege, conservatism, social stratification, and the solidarity of white people—at least those whites who shared the illusion of the subhumanity of black people.

Calhoun's political theory is symbolic of a special irony in American political thought. His doctrine of the "concurrent majority" is a powerful formulation of the rights of minorities and of their constant need of constitutional protection against what Alexis de Tocqueville called "the tyranny of the majority." Clearly, he makes a telling point: majorities are inclined to trample asunder the rights of minorities, and hence they must be restrained by organizations and instruments of power.

The problem is complex because the political system does not consist of a single minority but an endless variety of minorities—including subminorities of identifiable interest. Calhoun was only interested in the protection of a particular minority—and a particularly cruel and anti-democratic minority at that: the aristocratic, semi-feudal, slaveholding Southern minority against the majority of the nation, and maybe against the majority of the South itself.

Calhoun's formulation was designed and put forth with eloquence and skill to enable and to justify—indeed, to sanctify—the right of a regional minority to keep a racial minority in bondage. Thus, ironically, we have here an argument in behalf of the freedom and constitutional right of a white minority to keep a black minority in chains. Calhoun did not recognize the radical inconsistency, and in view of his racist presuppositions, there was none. Like others, he bifurcated the human order into white life and black life; he made the former superior, sacred, and an end in itself while the latter was made inferior, profane, and a tool for the former.

There is, however, still another irony fraught with possibilities. Ideas have a way of begetting a strange breed of children. Calhoun is "relevant" in a corrective, creative, and useful way to the Black Revolution. Perhaps this is a unique brand of poetic justice designed by the gods to mock the human condition. Substitute in his argument "black" for the aristocratic South, the interest he represented. Apply his doctrine of "concurrent majority" to the current racial predicament. Among the interesting conclusions is the necessity of a black veto on issues of public policy in order to promote and protect black interest. Add to the equation another Calhounian jewel: the plural executive. But, in this case, make one president black, another white, and the third an American Indian woman. Calhoun's doctrines of "interposition" and "nullification" may be viewed as conservative forms of "civil disobedience." He had other constitutional mechanisms to protect the vital interests of his minority, but the foregoing will do for now.

Calhoun emphasized the inclination of men of power to abuse and pervert power, to use it to their advantage and to the advantage of the interests they represent. Power alone is capable of restraining power. Hence, a minority is helpless and at the mercy of a majority with total power. Therefore, a given minority must be armed with the power of self-protection; it cannot leave the safety and advancement of its interest to the majority. Voting is an insufficient safeguard because the majority can always outvote the minority. In consequence, the minority must have veto power. This would overcome polarization and fragmentation among the citizens and create national consensus, unity, and order. It would also safeguard the public interest.

One of these days, Calhoun is going to be rediscovered, dusted off, updated, and used in the contemporary power and ideological struggles. He may well become purged and "blackized." If so, the political theory of the Black Revolution will be catalyzed, enlarged, and enriched. It would be the height of irony if the arguments advanced, prior to the Civil War, by the most gifted and influential apologist for black enslavement were converted, in the waning decades of the twentieth century, into arguments for black liberation. Ideas, sometimes, have strange careers, ambiguous legacies, and complex destinies—to the embarrassment and chagrin of their originators. Once afloat the continuum of history, they are free agents and often rebellious ones.

This country, for a variety of reasons, has not found it easy to square its liberal democratic ideals, promises, and pretensions with the agonizing and persistent realities of the aspirations of the black experience. Jefferson and Lincoln are, perhaps, the classic examples of this moral dilemma. Tortuous exercises in political thought have been commonplace. Manipulation of symbols, rationalizations, and corporate hyprocrisy have been pervasive and rampant, along with the side-stepping of basic issues. Vice has paid homage to virtue. This proposition is not to be taken lightly; for it suggests some of the ambiguity of the human condition in general, and the human condition in America in particular. Serious and sustained efforts were made—and not without success—to make the black encounter meaningless or "respectable" (that is, morally praiseworthy and democratically acceptable).

Profound contradictions of inner life and experience are, sometimes, hard to live with, particularly for the sensitive and good-will-motivated. The historic self-image of America is that of a pious, idealistic, and "Christian" country with a unique and divine mission in history: the burden of being mankind's best hope for achieving and spreading the blessings of human freedom, equality and dignity. Such a viewpoint represents about half of the reality of things.

Puritanism, with its vision of New Zion, moralism, individualism, the sovereignty of God in history, and purity of heart and conscience, has exerted a strong and continuing influence on the American mind and character. The faith of the Enlightenment—rationalism, equalitarianism, liberty, the progressive development of history, and human perfectibility—made its way, through Jefferson and others, into the American ethos. It has been a haunting reminder of human possibilities and social and political responsibilities. Above all was the influence of John Locke, who wrote eloquently about democracy, the social contract, the natural rights of man, and the free individual. He thus provided the New World with a model of a free society. Locke is the patron saint of American liberal democracy. As Louis Hartz has pointed out, even those who tried to repudiate him embraced him.[1] Locke prevailed.

America, then, inherited and affirmed certain ethical and political principles and ideals that are radically inconsistent with the black experience. The logic of the American Dream, as slaves knew intuitively, is incompatible with racial discrimination, injustice, oppression, and dehumanization. The methods and processes by which the country, for the most part, avoided honest self-confrontation are complex and ingenious. The price, however, was costly. It included a troubled conscience and a "split" personality for America—at least on the ultimate level. The integrity of the country's ideals and commitments was compromised and corrupted. As Hocking said, "the corruption of the best is the worst. . . ."[2] The feeling of moral self-betrayal is an awesome burden to bear, individually and collectively. It has been a terrible affliction for the political system, its citizens, and the moral and ethical presuppositions that inform and inspire both.

Deep inner contradictions create guilt and breed shame. In an odd twist of the moral economy and turn of the psychological wheel, they also foster self-righteousness, moral illusions, schizophrenia, and anguish of spirit. Men need, or appear to need, moral and psychological sanctions, a feeling of inner harmony and fidelity to basic values and commitments. Thus, concealment of reality in order to obscure or push beyond the field of vision and consciousness various infirmities, failures and shortcomings, are typical tactics of individuals, groups, nations. Self-confrontation can be a painful experience. It can generate sickness of heart and torment the spirit. No wonder many of us conceive the Socratic injunction to "know thyself" as a violation of our natural, moral, and constitutional rights and obligations.

America, in the context of the black experience, has developed and elevated pretensions to the status of a fine art. But the desperate need to feign virtue is, perhaps, partial evidence of the *ultimate* decency of certain men and societies. Truly evil men and nations have no such need except for narrow and immediate self-serving propagandistic and manipulative purposes. America is morally ambiguous precisely because of the profound need to be pretentious and hypocritical about the treatment of black people. It has desperately sought self-consistency, harmony, and peace with its democratic and humanistic ideals. The inner struggle has been difficult, intense, and complex.

Beneath the surface, America has not had an easy or complacent conscience about racial injustice and oppression. The largest and most costly civil war fought by the country has been on the battlefield of the inner life of the divided national self. This moral, psychological, and emotional warfare has been continuous and destructive. Rationalizations and other defense mechanisms have been too glib, elaborate, compulsive, monotonous, anguished, and persistent to emanate from an easy conscience. They betray self-doubt, a troubled conscience, a divided self. Just as the slave masters depicting slaves as happy and loyal to them displayed a paranoic fear of desertions, insurrections, rebellions, and conspiracies, America, celebrating the democracy, equality, and freedom of the New World, was engaged in furious and endless attempts at moral and political purgation and justification about the fateful lot of black men. Nagging doubt could not be erased; inner torment could not be assuaged; the specter of the American Dream refused to stop haunting.

The self-cleansing was dishonest and hence futile, and the consistencies were forced and tortuous, but the capacity and need, perhaps, disclose higher and creative moral, social, and political possibilities. Ambiguities can be resolved in creative, humane, and inclusive terms as well as destructive, inhuman, and exclusive terms. The hope and destiny of the land depend on how the nation resolves the ambiguity of its attitude and behavior toward black Americans.

The defense of slavery began with an apologetic view of it as a "necessary evil" and ended up with the assertion that it was a "positive good," even for the dehumanized and brutalized slaves robbed of political and constitutional rights and moral autonomy. The ambiguous conscience of the country required either that slavery be completely abolished or that the institution of slavery be "moralized" and slaves completely dehumanized. The latter was the tragic course taken, but the democratic, humanistic, and idealistic impulses of the land, after much anguish and struggle, reversed the course. Slavery collapsed, but racial injustice continued in different forms and on new levels of being.

The North assented to slavery and other brutish forms of institutional racism, in part, because of the worthy impulses toward national "unity," interest, social peace and harmony, consensus, compromise, and stability. The fact that these were tragic illusions is not central to the legitimacy of the impulses. Moral ambiguities tend to be an ally of the established order of injustice and oppression. Who wants to glorify national disorder, instability, and chaos? Throughout American history, black life has been tragically victimized by the perversion of democracy, humanism, and other worthy social ideals. The first and last values to be subordinated and sacrificed in the public calculus of competitive options and priorities have been those of black men. The motives, of course, have been complex and mixed. Injustice and oppression have a way of masquerading as justice and freedom.

It is only fair that the Abolitionists and their descendants, on the whole, understood the score. They stressed the sovereignty and directive power of liberal democratic ideals and the incompatibility of racism with them. William Lloyd Garrison's denunciation of the Constitution because it sanctioned slavery is an eloquent reminder. Even so, few of the Abolitionists really believed in, or were committed to, the equality of black men as citizens and as human beings—equality in its total dimensions for black people. Racism has corrupted the mind, spirit, and conscience of the country so deeply that many "liberal" and even "radical" whites have had reservations about black humanity beyond the minimal level of emancipation and strict "civil rights." The self-imposed qualifications of many of today's white liberals on black humanity are a grim reminder of the depth and persistence of racism.

American political thought and experience sought to resolve the dilemma of the coexistence of black oppression and the liberal democratic creed of the country by denying the reality of the contradiction at the level of definition and conception. Selective views of democracy and constitutionalism were developed and refined with "scholarly detachment" and "erudition." Apologists for slavery invoked the Greek ideal of democracy to "prove" not only the compatibility of slavery and democracy but to "demonstrate" that slavery was a necessary condition of democracy. Of course, since black men were not human, so the argument went, white men had no moral, social, and political obligation to them. For the South at least, the bondage of black men was conceived as a basis of the freedom of white men.

Integrally related to the problem of the experiential reality of the Negro in the American liberal democratic tradition is the issue of his treatment by social scientists and other commentators on American thought and experience. Two basic frameworks, therefore, need overhauling and perhaps revolutionizing—the level of political existence and the level of political inquiry. These two levels are interactive and interdependent; they constitute a single continuum of theory and practice.

Unconsciously no doubt, American political science, despite its heavy emphasis on empiricism, behavioralism, and realism, has not done justice to the harsh treatment of the black political experience. It has been guided by categories, perceptions, interpretations, and applications which have not reflected the unsavory facts surrounding the status of blacks within the political system. These frames of meaning are not in themselves racist; they are, rather, tacit and unwitting vehicles of racism because of the manner of conceptualization and application.

Of commanding significance are the network of suppressed value judgments and implicit assumptions under the confident and self-propelling guise of a "value-free" methodology. Such inquiries are, however, "value-laden" instead of "value-free." They become the insidious instrument of the values and assumptions of the status quo.

The categories and presuppositions, generally speaking, contain built-in filters that automatically block off significant sectors of experience, selecting certain phenomena to the exclusion of others. They are self-feeding and self-perpetuating—paralleling and reinforcing the racist character of political life. Thus, the empiricism and realism of American political science are not empirical and realistic enough; the idealism of the discipline is not sufficiently idealistic, and the behavioral school fails to come to grips with the total behavior and workings of the political system.

Political scientists, for example, use such categories as pluralism, liberalism, democracy, freedom, equality, political change, representation, civic culture, constitutionalism, consensus, electorate, public opinion, and public policy, without any significant reference to the brute and embarrassing realities of the black experience. The black political encounter is not taken seriously. For example, how does the reality of the black political experience affect and limit the functioning and success of pluralism, democracy, liberalism, stability, and so on? What are the relationships—the gulfs—between model and objective reality? What qualifications must be made to do justice both to the methodological categories and to the phenomena they are designed to analyze and illuminate? Too much of political science is indeed irrelevant to blacks and hence to significant aspects of the totality of the behavioral or empirical actualities of the political system and governmental process. Black men have been alienated not only from the realities, rewards, and benefits of the American political system but from the governing categories and presuppositions of political science as well.

The problem is, therefore, fundamental. For often

the very categories and presuppositions of political science itself are psychologically, institutionally, and methodologically rigged—so cleverly that the uncomfortable realities of the black experience are made invisible, insignificant, or nonexistent. They have taken on the property of the self-evident and the self-perpetuating, which means black exclusion from meaningful consideration and exploration of the political system.

When a large and significant segment of the population is inequitably treated, in terms of both input and output by the political system, the result has profound meaning and consequences for the democratic ideal. Democracy means something in terms of the distribution and responsibility of power, the enjoyment of human rights, and the experience of freedom and equality. The meaning and character of democracy are defiled by the oppression of men. If a significant minority is oppressed, the reality of democracy is to that degree negated; hence distinctions and qualifications are necessary to do justice to the premise and promise of democracy and to the oppressed group. Democracy, as ideal and principle, is always a matter of degree, because of the ever-present realm of higher possibilities which beckons men.

Higher possibilities, however, are rationally impossible in terms of means-end relationships, if defects are denied, performance falsified, and perceptions distorted. Creative tension between the "is" and the "ought" is a moral imperative of the democratic way of conducting the public's business and managing the citizen's vital interests. Injustice, not justice, is done to the democratic cause when too much is claimed for its concrete achievements in the drama of history.

As with democracy, so it is with pluralism, constitutionalism, liberalism, equality, freedom, and so on. The degree of these attributes makes a significant difference in the quality of political life and hence in the treatment and evaluation of that life. Their value is demeaned by an exaggeration or tacit assumption of their reality in public life.

Much of the defect of political science in dealing with the reality of the black experience in the political system is due to a messianic commitment to a value-free methodology. Social science is, at best, only semi-value-free. Values are inescapable in dealing with men (individually and collectively) and social and political phenomena. On the ultimate level man as a seeker of knowledge is inseparable from man as a bearer of values. The myth of value-free political science means, in effect, scientific sanctification and perpetuation of the racist status quo of the political system. It supports and sustains blind categories, insensitive presuppositions, and humanistically and operationally sterile structures of meaning.

Essential, then, is a reconstruction not necessarily of the categories and presuppositions themselves but of their use, meaning, and significance—the development of a new consciousness and sensitivity to the stubborn and brute reality of things as they relate to the black political experience. It might be necessary in some cases to revise and extend the categories and presuppositions themselves. Their conformity with reality is not important: that is impossible. What is significant is the relationship between these categories and reality, and the yawning gulf between them. It is necessary to have a more careful and exhaustive critical evaluation of the reality of political phenomena. Imperative, too, are the making of implicit judgments of value explicit, a more careful elaboration of the limits and possibilities of the democratic ideal in light of the factual character of the political system, and the exploration of alternative possibilities.

There is evidence that the situation is changing. The black political experience is finally being "discovered" and made the object of serious investigation like the other realities of American political life. It will not help much, though, if the black political experience is studied in isolation, apart from the larger realities and presuppositions of the political system. The reality and aspirations of blacks must be integrated into the basic elements of American political science. To the extent that blacks are made invisible and ignored, to that degree the political system is not functioning properly. And, correspondingly, unless political science takes the defects of the political system seriously, it is not dealing adequately with the realities and possibilities of political life. Both will be guilty of the charge of "irrelevance" to the lives of black people. Since the black minority constitutes about 11 percent of the total population and ranks with Indians as the most ancient and loyal Americans, its status is fraught with significance, meaning, and consequences for the vitality of the liberal democratic tradition, the viability of the political system, and the integrity of political science. Blacks can no longer be ignored or theoretically converted into meaningless and nonexistent phenomena.

In a famous passage of his classic, *Democracy in America*, Tocqueville, the brilliant French observer of the American scene in the early 1830s, asserted: "The great advantage of the Americans is that they have arrived at a state of democracy without having to endure a democratic revolution, and that they are born equal instead of becoming so." This is the typical view of the American condition: Americans are born free and equal; democracy is a "given" of historical experience, an inherited quality of things; there is no need, therefore, for a democratic revolution. It is an absolute absurdity to seek and to struggle for a self-evident inheritance of principles, premises, institutions, and other conditions of freedom and equality. What is essential is the glorification, celebration, and preservation of the richness and wonders of democratic and equalitarian grace.

Another Tocquevillian observation has had wide currency. Tocqueville was not only struck by what he perceived as the principle of equality but the "equality of condition in the land." This equality of condition, he wrote, "is the fundamental fact from which all others seem to be derived and the central point at which all my observations constantly terminated."[3] This assertion is symbolic of the tragically selective, restrictive, and misleading character of general observations on American public life. It unites illusion and reality, and the disentanglement of the two is not easy without a fresh and more inclusive perspective and a deeper grasp of the factual landscape of the liberal democratic tradition.

Tocqueville and others who have celebrated the sovereignty of the liberal democratic tradition in America had only some, not all, Americans in mind. They had white people, not black people, as the focus of attention. (Indians, of course, were excluded, too, and there have been other grave disabilities.) Alongside his observations on "born equal," democracy, and "equality of condition" were very perceptive and prophetic comments on the nature and consequences of slavery and the experiences of oppression of "free" Negroes in the North.

But he did not see the profound implications and consequences of the latter for the former. The presence of slavery meant the absence of democracy or, at least, the radical corruption and perversion of democracy. Injustice and oppression always limit, modify, and demean the character of democratic institutions. It is terribly important to make the necessary distinctions and qualifications and to identify the degree and kind of democracy. Democracy and liberalism for whom?

The conclusion that black men have been, for the most part, outside the performance and ethos of the liberal tradition in America—in terms of the premises, norms, and promises of that tradition—is inescapable. From the perspective of the black experience, the liberal tradition is an exciting and tragic illusion. America was indeed "settled by men fled from the feudal and clerical oppressions of the Old World," but the New World developed, sanctified, and perpetuated its own pathetic brand of human oppression—racial.

The New World has a romanticized and moralized self-image which has enabled it to conceal from itself some harsh and brutal facts of life. The illusion has been self-feeding and self-perpetuating. Freedom, equality, and democracy have been assumed not only as self-evident norms but as self-evident facts. It has been almost impossible to break through and transcend this intoxicating and self-satisfying illusion. Hartz comments that "I have been interpreting the social thought of the American revolution in terms of social goals *it did not need to achieve.*"[4] Thus freedom, equality, and democracy are a birthright and empirical reality—for white people. Basically, liberal democracy has been perceived as a white prerogative and inheritance.

Hartz insists that owing to the sovereignty of the

"liberal tradition" (which itself is due to the absence of feudalism and hence of the need to mount a democratic revolution to overthrow feudal institutions), America has neither a genuine radical and revolutionary tradition, nor a genuine conservative and reactionary tradition. It also lacks, in his view, a "crusading spirit." The American experience does not contain the agonies and tragedies of the Old World; hence, it lacks millennialism and "civic religion." He puts it this way:

> Europe's brilliant dream of an impending millennium, like the mirage of a thirst-ridden man, was inspired in large part by the agonies it experienced. When men have already inherited the freest society in the world, and are grateful for it, their thinking is bound to be of a solider type.[5]

The miseries and tragedies of blacks have been obscured and moralized by mythology, ethos, and rhetoric. The black experience is the chief link between the oppressions of the Old World and the New. Perhaps the major difference is that the tyranny of the Old World was recognized as such (at least by most of the enlightened and sensitive), but the tyranny of the New, as experienced by black people, is called democracy, liberalism, equality, and freedom. This makes it all the more difficult to topple. There is indeed no need for a "democratic revolution" if the prior assumption is made of the objective existence and vitality of democracy.

Within a few years, our country will be celebrating its bicentenary. It will have much to celebrate. It will also have, however, much to contemplate and to be remorseful about. The "Spirit of '76" has yet to touch and to embrace, at the deeper levels of experience, the lives of black people. The bicentennial celebration will be a good time for soul-searching, revitalizing, renewing, and rededicating ourselves to the ideals and promises of the land. But can a country that accepts the mythology of its citizens being "born free and equal" be realistic and honest enough to admit to itself that, for all these years, a large segment of its population has not participated in, and reaped the benefits of, the rightful inheritance of the soil? Is it possible for the vast majority of Americans who were "born free" to recognize and appreciate the oppressions experienced by its black minority? Can the New World understand that its racial oppressions are as tragic as the clerical and feudal oppressions of the Old? Can it bring itself to understand that black men have been deprived of their birthright by that very liberal democratic tradition which is so unique in the history of Western civilization?

The lineage between the American Revolution and the Black Revolution is direct, clear, and sure. The Black Revolution is about what America, at its best, is about: democracy, freedom, equality, and dignity. Since black men (Tocqueville's observation notwithstanding) have not arrived at "a state of democracy," they have to go through a democratic revolution; since they were not "born equal" in accordance with the imperatives and traditions of the country, they must "become so." Whites have inherited their rights; blacks have to win theirs. The Black Revolution is the struggle of black men for incorporation in the liberal democratic enterprise and tradition of the country. It is a declaration of independence from an oppressed existence and a demand for diplomatic recognition and equal membership in the community of liberal democracy.

The Black Revolution, then, is the legitimate and necessary expression of the American Dream. Tocqueville was prophetic; he sensed something of the inevitability of the revolt of black people against the yoke of oppression. "If," he said, "ever America undergoes great revolutions, they will be brought about by the presence of the black race on the soil of the United States; that is to say, they will owe their origin, not to the equality, but to the inequality of condition."[6]

Martin Luther King, Jr. was more than the principal leader, catalyst, architect, and prophet of the Black Revolution; he was a chief theorist and interpreter of it as well. He occupies a special place in the annals of black history and ranks among the foremost public figures and inspiring moral leaders produced by the New World. In a profound sense, he was to the Black Revolution what Washington was to the birth of the nation, Jefferson to the American Revolution and the liberal democratic tradition, Jackson to the frontier farmer and city worker, Calhoun to the aristocratic slaveholders, Lenin to the Russian Revolution, and Gandhi to Indian independence. All the others held high public office with immense built-in advantages of various stable and continuing sources of power, influence, and privilege. King was a private citizen. He had only the power of persuasion, and history did not give him much time. He was particularly gifted at moving men and events; he could disturb the human conscience.

The social and political philosophy of Dr. King was built on the solid rock of the existential character of the American liberal, humanistic, idealistic, and democratic tradition, with its capacity for growth, renewal, and extension to the world of higher possibilties and more inclusive realities. He believed the resources and potential of that tradition were mighty; he had profound and abiding faith in the creative and redemptive possibilities of the land he loved. Accordingly, in his majestic and powerful appeal to the best in America to get rid of the worst in America, Dr. King combined traditionalism and militant nonviolent commitment to radical social and political reform, realism and idealism, the ethics of power, and the power of ethics. With the skill of a surgeon and a prophet's passion for social justice and righteousness, he dug into the tangled roots of national existence. He articulated the aspirations and anguish of the wounded and oppressed. He looked outward and inward grasping the heights and the depths, the misery and the dignity of the nation's self.

The basis of Dr. King's dream and practical efforts was a model of simplicity: to make the American Dream as relevant, meaningful, and applicable to black Americans as to white Americans. He looked beyond the darkness of current reality to the light of limitless possibilities; beyond the chaos, injustice, and division of "being" to the ordered liberty and equality, justice, and unity of "becoming."

The political philosophy of Martin Luther King, Jr. is about the unity and continuum of morality, power, and social change. His goal was simple enough: social and economic justice, which is necessary to the creation of the beloved community. Dr. King's method was, in essence, that of creative encounter and constructive tension. The former entails American self-confrontation at the basic level of meaning, conception, and purpose; a face-to-face dialogue between ideal and reality, promise and fulfillment. The latter refers to the difficult struggles with strategic centers of power. The purpose of the first was to sensitize and catalyze the nation, mobilize its will, modify its climate, and reorder its priorities. The purpose of the second was to alter the power relations of the marketplace.

Dr. King saw clearly the perversions, corruptions, and perils inherent in making the American Creed restrictive. He grasped the essential dimensions of the destructive tension stemming from the gulf between promise and performance in the American Dream. He also recognized the ethical and social resources embedded in it and in the country, and he developed a methodology for using these resources to bring about a better society.

Dr. King was unsurpassed in the mastery of the tragic incongruities and jarring contradictions at the heart of American life and culture. He understood the deep and perilous ambivalence of white America toward black America in all dimensions of racism—institutional, personal, and ultimate.

In a sad and ironic way, Martin Luther King, Jr.'s dream was the American Dream eloquently expressing itself through the ancient and alien grievances and tragic experiences which the liberal democratic tradition confidently thought it left buried forever in the cemetery of historical memories of the feudal and clerical oppressions of the Old World. It is somewhat strange and incredible music to American ears. A predominantly liberal bourgeois culture, however, always finds it difficult to recognize and cope with collective human tragedy. Such a culture is addicted to excessive optimism and thus tends to exaggerate its achievements. Therefore, it is inclined to be blind and insensitive to brute realities that do not fit its self-image and preconceptions. The deadly illusion that the triumph of American liberalism signaled a benediction to oppression, since it was allegedly limited to the Old World, obscured and sanctified enclaves of oppression in the household of the very citadel of liberalism—oppression no less real and poignant because of its relegation to the attic or basement.

Noting the moral schizophrenia of the New World, Dr. King said:

> Ever since the birth of our nation, white America has had a schizophrenic personality on the question of race. She has been torn between selves—a self in which she proudly professed the great principles of democracy and a self in which she sadly practiced the antithesis of democracy. This tragic duality has produced a strange indecisiveness and ambivalence toward the Negro, causing America to take a step backward simultaneously with every step forward on the question of racial justice, to be at once attracted to the Negro and repelled by him, to love and to hate him. There has never been a solid, unified and determined thrust to make justice a reality for Afro-Americans.[7]

Dr. Walton's book is a unique achievement. It is, to my knowledge, the first systematic and comprehensive account of the political philosophy of Martin Luther King, Jr. Since being "the first" is not necessarily a virtue, I must quickly add that the book has genuine merit independent of temporal priority and seniority. It is an impressive performance and a significant contribution not only to the literature about Dr. King and the Black Revolution, but also to contemporary social and political theories of historical change.

This book is a description, analysis, and critical evaluation of the major ideas and contributions of Dr. King to the wonderful enterprise of philosophizing about government and politics. Men, no doubt, will be wrestling with Dr. King's ideas for a long time. Although he spoke primarily to the American version of the human predicament with its cancer of racism, his crucial ideas transcend time, place, and race. They speak, in the final analysis, of the basic issues of the human journey; of what John Dewey called the "problems of men." They combine particularism and universalism, the timely and the timeless. Racial injustice is only one form of human oppression, and racism is only one expression of the problem of collective human relationships. Collective pride, egotism, and self-love are perennial problems of the human condition; they manifest themselves in a variety of ways. There are universal elements in Dr. King's social and political philosophy. The American scene was simply their point of departure and immediate frame of reference. Ultimately, Dr. King was dealing with the problems of justice, freedom, order, and community—problems at the heart of the whole corpus of the history of social and political philosophy. He succeeds.

If the future explorations and probings of Dr. King's ideas bear fruit, Dr. Walton's book may well be a significant contributing factor. He raises many critical issues and is not afraid to make controversial value judgments and to take unpopular stands. He seeks neither to glorify nor to downgrade Dr. King but to understand, examine, and assess his ideas and contributions.

Perhaps a personal note will be forgiven—in terms of the normal boredom and curse of human vanity. Martin Luther King, Jr. was a dear friend and college classmate of mine. I unabashedly revere his friendship, contributions, and memory. Hanes Walton, Jr. is a former student of mine. He is also a good friend, and I admire his scholarly productivity and boundless intellectual industry. Thus, despite the innocuous "clash of loyalties," I am doubly proud and privileged to write this introductory essay, in which I roam all over the forest.

In reading the manuscript, there were times when I wanted to heap excessive praise on my former student for his erudition and insight, but there were also times when I, in the face of his relentless analysis and critical evaluation, wanted to defend my ol' classmate, M. L. (M. L. is what most of us called Dr. King in college.) The reader will, perhaps, understand my ambivalence, but he is likely to underestimate my joy and inner delight. My only regret is that M. L., who loved to discuss and to debate great ideas, is not around for his gracious, perceptive, and tolerant rejoinder to Dr. Walton. But such is the imperative of the human condition. We have our say and others theirs. Ultimate silence is our common fate. Life, including life of the mind, goes on. It must.

SAMUEL DuBOIS COOK
THE FORD FOUNDATION

NOTES

1. Louis Hartz, *The Liberal Tradition in America* (New York: Harcourt, Brace and World, Inc., 1955).
2. William E. Hocking, *Man and the State* (New Haven: Yale University Press, 1926), p. 441.
3. Alexis de Tocqueville, *Democracy in America,* trans. Henry Reeve and ed. Phillips Bradley (New York: Vintage Books, 1966), I, 108.
4. Hartz, *Liberal Tradition in America,* p. 50.
5. Hartz, *Liberal Tradition in America,* p. 39.
6. Tocqueville, *Democracy in America,* p. 270.
7. Martin Luther King, Jr., *Where Do We Go From Here: Chaos or Community?* (New York: Bantam Books, 1968), p. 80.

THE POLITICAL PHILOSOPHY OF
MARTIN LUTHER KING, JR.

1 | *The Function of Political Theory*

SOCIAL, economic, and political philosophies are of necessity based on certain assumptions regarding the nature of man. Reasons and justifications for these assumptions, no matter how convincingly presented, stand little chance of altering the habitual thoughts and behavior of people unless they command the attention of a significant audience. For this to happen, for a philosophy to come alive in our daily world, it must depend upon the persuasiveness and character of those who speak for it, on the force of leaders who seem to embody that of which they speak.

Martin Luther King, Jr. was such a leader, a theorist and a crusader whose successes and failures can only be properly measured in relation to the historical time in which he played a vital part. Society changes as ideas are born and reborn, as theories wed and clash over issues and points of departure that continuously rise anew. No thought exists in a vacuum, and political thought especially is wrought from the elements of conflict: those existing within a society or between societies, from the struggle between what is and what ought to be, out of the contest for power and authority; from the interaction of all of these forces, systematic political thought is eventually distilled.

The primary concern of political theory is the problem of the distribution and control of power between individuals and groups. It compels thinking men to ask the question "to what purpose is man's life, and his life within a given society?" Although the focus of most political discussion is upon the normative, descriptive, and causative aspects of politics, it is apparent that a clear statement of any one aspect of a political problem implies a set of ideas related to every other aspect.

To come alive, to be acted upon, political thought must be capable of interacting with the prevailing social values, whatever their source and history. Conditioned by the social ideas of a period, and in turn attempting to condition those existing ideas, political theories aim to provide a basis for increasingly enlightened political action and a healthier social body.

In any period, political philosophies can be defined as either supportive or critical of the existing institutions and methods of the state. According to Professor Leo Strauss, "political things are by their nature subject to approval or disapproval, to choice and rejection, to praise and blame. It is of their essence not to be neutral, but to raise claim to men's obedience, decision, or judgment."[1]

Because political thought is concerned with those rules of action in a society which are or should be enforced, and the reasons for this, the search for ultimate values in the political sphere is continuous.[2] Concretely, this means that full human rights can exist only in a reasonably stable society. When the cohesion of a society is threatened, liberty degenerates into license and government either loses its authority or must act more aggressively to retain it. At this point anarchy may become more than just a threat. Since a measure of political stability is a precondition of individual liberty, society is organized with a governing body enabled to enforce rules of action. Our government maintains itself and regulates its own changes through laws which it is prepared to back up by force. Since, however, what may be generally accepted as necessary for political stability may not be best for the individual, it is the concern of the political philosopher to fashion a better system to provide for both stability and change and to help shape the optimum direction of change.

According to their manner of conceiving and providing for stability and change, political philosophies can be classified as either conservative or critical. Conservative theories attempt to justify the existing political system in all its positive aspects, and, fundamentally, to maintain the status quo. The politically good and right is identified with the present or a past system; to change which would be to risk chaos, anarchy, or all that, in the name of civilization, has thus far been secured.

Theories critical of the prevailing form of government may support various kinds of changes and various means of change to differing degrees. Critical reformers are, generally, fired by moral outrage at the injustices of the given system and by a vision, however dimly perceived, of a better world.

Martin Luther King, Jr., guided by a vision of a "beloved community" on earth, was a social critic of the sort whose role in relation to society was classically stated by the fifth-century teacher and founder of political philosophy, Socrates, who, when accused by the Athenian government of introducing new gods and of corrupting the youth, defended himself by saying:

And now, Athenians, I am not going to argue for my own sake, as you may think, but for yours, that you

may not sin against the God by condemning me, who
am his gift to you. For if you kill me, who if I may use
such a ludicrous figure of speech, am a sort of gadfly,
given to the State by God; and the State is a great and
noble steed who is tardy in motions oweing to his very
size and requires to be stirred into life. I am that gadfly which God has attached to the State, and all day
long and in all places am always fastening upon you,
arousing and persuading and reproaching you. You
will not easily find another like me, and therefore I
would advise you to spare me.[3]

This magnificent statement is as valid and as reveal-
ing today as it was when it was first framed. What
Socrates is telling us is that society—any society—tends
to become smug, sluggish, and unthinkingly set in its
ways. It must be "stirred into life" if constructive
changes are to be made. This job of stirring up is the
function of the "gadfly," or social critic, whose "bite" is,
of course, likely to be annoying. There will be citizens
who will resent the social critic and may even demand
that he be silenced, while others will be stimulated into
thinking about conditions and proposals that might
otherwise have never come to their attention. From
criticism a new dialogue may begin and, ultimately, a
new trend in public opinion develop.

King's political thought was primarily critical, aimed
at explaining and denouncing the evils within the present system and finding ways to rectify them. He sought
to convince the American people of the "rightness" of
his political convictions, if they were to move toward
what he held to be the good life. If he stressed a particular public policy it was because he felt that it would
achieve justice. While not denouncing the American
system of government, he condemned those practices al-

lowed by the system which are not consistent with its pronounced ideals. His theory was designed to make the ideals of American society genuinely operative by eliminating the contradictions between the convictions expressed in this country's Constitution and the actions permitted to take place in the South against a racial minority.

Central to King's political thought is the concept of the role that the black man must play in elevating himself. Just as Rousseau's concept of the general will, Plato's concept of the philosopher King, Hobbes' and Locke's concept of the social contract, and Saint Augustine's concept of original sin, are crucial to an understanding of their philosophies, so too is King's concept of the blacks' "saving" mission in America the keystone to his political edifice. The reasons for this derive from those distinct features characterizing the black man's situation in America: he belongs to a minority defined by its color and one with no realistic hope of becoming a majority, and hence lacking the basic right of minorities built into the definition of democracy, namely, the right to try to become a majority. King's definition of the American Negro's role is one aimed at securing the social, economic, and political institutionalization of freedom denied him by the majority. To accomplish this, the minority must prod the government into action while, at the same time, it must outline a policy whereby the government could extend to its minorities their full political rights.

Wholly accepting of the constitutional framework of this country, King always attempted to stay within its laws and, wherever possible, to use the law to gain the black man's basic rights. To attain his objectives, King employed tactics intended to precipitate a legal case, wherein local, state, and regional provisions for integration would be finally confronted. The most effective means for creating a crisis situation which would force a formerly adamant community to confront an issue was, King felt, nonviolent direct action in tandem with legal pressures. The combination of these two forces could bring about what neither of them could if used alone.

What King's political theory seeks to do is to restructure the conflictful situation by means of ethical techniques intended to alter the attitudes of the antagonists. The resolution of conflicts through peaceful means would enable the American people—blacks and whites—to move closer to what King called the beloved community, or the good life. By the use of nonviolent means, the end result would be much more complete and lasting.

It was up to blacks to make a bold and brave start towards the ideals reflected in the Preamble of the Constitution, in the Constitution itself, the Bill of Rights, and the Thirteenth, Fourteenth, and Fifteenth Amendments. To do this, he felt blacks needed a powerful sense of determination to remove the blemish of racism that was "defiling American democracy and keeping it from achieving the ultimate ideal as the grandest form of government ever conceived by the minds of men."

The issue, in King's mind, was momentous and the contest not an easy one. Nonviolent gadflies were needed to create the kind of tension in our society that Socrates created in his, so that the individual could rise from the "dark depths of prejudice and racism to the majestic heights of understanding and brotherhood." Commenting on King's strategy, Samuel Lubell stated that his aim was to demonstrate that segregation could be maintained only by constant police repression. This, Lubell felt, would embarrass the national leaders and assail the national conscience, forcing negotiation on the local level, or federal intervention and an acceleration on civil rights on the national level.[4]

In order to understand the genesis and context of King's political ideas it is necessary to look, if only briefly, at the history of the black man in the United States, a history of which King felt himself to be a part and a continuation. The deeper our understanding of the times in which he lived, the greater our comprehension of the man, and of the times in which we are living today.

In treating the broad historical background of the movement toward freedom which King inherited, our object is not to detail all of the theories and ideologies that have surfaced, but something of the growth of those ideas which have particularly affected the political fate of the black minority in America.

NOTES

Complete bibliographic information for abbreviated references is given in the Bibliography.

1. Strauss, *What Is Political Philosophy*, p. 12.
2. Hyneman, *Study of Politics*, p. 120.
3. Jowett, trans., *The Dialogues of Plato*, pp. 335–36.
4. Lubell, *White and Black*, pp. 103–4.

2 | *Early Paths to Freedom: Actions and Theory*

> Every great period of social change in American history has been set off by the demand of some excluded but aggressive group for larger participation in the national democracy; in the age of Jackson by the frontier farmer, the city worker, the small entrepreneur; in the Progressive era by the by-passed old upper classes of the cities; in the New Deal by labor in mass production industries, the unemployed and the intellectuals. The uprising of the Negroes now contained the potentiality of ushering in a new era which would not only win Negroes their rights but renew the democratic commitment of the national community.[1]

THE AMERICAN egalitarian and so-called open society has, since 1661, when the first black petition for freedom was recorded, witnessed a continual struggle for the rights of a minority group denied full human status because of its color. Since their arrival in this country and their subsequent enslavement, the black minority has sought by whatever means it could, to achieve the justice and equality envisaged in this nation's fundamental credo for all its citizens.

To clarify what is generally meant today by the term social justice, we may begin by defining it as the body of legal and moral rules, statutes or precedents, written or unwritten, which a society upholds. A society, if it is to call itself just, must treat, in both its formal and informal actions, similar cases similarly and all citizens on a like human basis, while yet respecting their inevitable differences in capacities, needs, contribution, and merit. By implication, a society which does not by its own initiative attempt to bring about the greatest possible measure of justice, is tacitly violating a moral principle; for justice and morality are rooted in the same profound sense of what is right for man. It follows that social justice must extend beyond the bare requirements of legal equality to a respect for the intrinsic dignity and value of each human life and concern for the quality of people's lives. An egalitarian spirit—which need not presume the material equality of citizens—is as vital to a democracy as are its laws. A brief look at some of the different kinds of equality may be useful for bearing in mind the broad terrain included under this general concept.

Political equality may be defined as having an effective share in the decisions that shape the institutions of the community. Civil or legal equality allows for a measure of control over the conditions by which one participates in the community, i.e., in the choice of religion, the expression of opinions, the right of assembly and petition, the right to associations of one's choice, the right to serve on juries, and so forth. Economic equality implies the absence of discrimination based on factors other than a person's abilities and qualifications for a job, in addition to equal opportunity for education, technical training, and personal development. By moral equality we mean the spiritual equality of people as free human beings. But any attempt to classify types of equality will inevitably reveal how inseparable they are on any functional level. Any political movement aimed at bringing about greater social equality will involve these and still other areas of life. The drive for greater racial equality, one of the most complex and significant of all the movements toward an egalitarian democratic society, illustrates at every stage how interdependent all aspects of equality actually are.

The Negro, because of his initially deprived status in this country, has been in the unique position of having to try to attain each and every form of equality, sometimes many at once. Consequently, his political movements have had to become increasingly diversified.

In colonial times his status as slave—except for a tiny proportion of free Negroes—meant that he had none of the ordinary civil and personal rights of a citizen. Nor was that the extent of his depredation: American slavery "was profoundly different from, and in its lasting effects on individuals and their children indescribably worse than, any recorded servitude, ancient or modern." Though some of the slaves brought to the Americas may have known slavery in their own lands, it was a condition imposed by a victorious tribe upon members of the losing tribe, and therefore based not on color but on superior might. If he could manage to escape, the defeated African would have his freedom back. Running away had been the Negro's chief way of resisting oppression in Africa, and this was the sole response he brought with him to the Americas. Colonial America saw numerous breakaways that were the natural, instinctive reaction of slaves to their condition. These revolts had no abstract frame of reference; they were rooted in traditional practice and sheer necessity.

With the growth of humanitarian ideas, particularly among religious groups, and the flowering of revolutionary thought in America, the picture began to change.

Many blacks in the North were freed, sometimes due to an economic structure which did not rely upon an embonded labor force, sometimes due to state legislation, and sometimes as the private act of slaveholders wanting to purge their consciences. Blacks might also be freed for having shown dedication, or for having performed outstanding or heroic acts of service for their masters or country.

Still, these northern blacks were a long way from being free men, facing as they did, economic, social, and political discrimination in every form. It was the free blacks of the North who were the first to feel the pains of a segregated society. Yet, a right to education did exist, and many slaveholders in the North, both before and after manumitting their slaves, made attempts to provide them with an education of sorts. Usually this was no more than rudimentary instruction, sufficient to run a household or a business. Schools for blacks were established in some northern states, and in others they were permitted to attend white schools. Before long the first black college graduate appeared, schools were named after blacks and taught by blacks for blacks. Once a sizeable number of blacks had received an education they passed this learning on to others, through town meetings, conventions, and publications. With freedom came increased education and with education came ideas and the development of theories to rationalize and support further moves toward liberation.

Basing their arguments on the principles of the Declaration of Independence, the Constitution, religious dogma, and belief in the innate rights of man, the free blacks in the North began to attack discrimination. Opposition to oppression began relating its cause to the theoretical framework of the humanist tradition and, by

1829, when David Walker read his appeal to the slaves of the South, he could call upon them to revolt and destroy the slavocracy on the grounds that their inherent rights had been denied them.

In the ante bellum South, the situation determined that the path to freedom take a more laborious and painful route. Prior to the invention of the cotton gin, the manumission of slaves had begun to take place, albeit haltingly. By 1800 Negro restlessness had enhanced doubts among slave owners and southerners concerning the wisdom of slavery. Still, no southern state made any notable effort to pass legislation liberating slaves. The agricultural dependency of the South, the invention of the cotton gin, and the rise of "king cotton" cut short whatever tendencies there may have been to free slaves. As slavery became increasingly profitable for the owners of large plantations, the institution itself became sacrosanct and the grounds for justifying it multiplied.[2]

Free southern blacks had, prior to the more rigid institutionalization and proliferation of slavery, begun to lay claim to a modicum of education. Schools were established in several southern cities, and when, after outright slave revolts these were banned, they went underground.[3] Southern slaves fared even less well. Though a select few were given special training as artisans and craftsmen, generally education was limited to the productive skills needed to run the plantation; occasionally literacy was encouraged out of the kindness of an owner Most of what passed for education was religious study which fostered the passive virtues that served the master as a means of social control. But it was with the rudiments of this religious education that southern blacks, free and slave, were able to begin to construct theories with which to bolster and justify their resistance. Not enough is known about the beginnings of rationalized opposition used by free blacks in the South, but some insight is afforded by an examination of petitions sent to state legislatures requesting relief from grievances and presenting arguments buttressed with religious references.[4]

Little, too, is known about the racial consciousness of the southern free blacks, but there is on record the case of Denmark Vesey, who for several years agitated for insurrection among the slaves of Charleston, South Carolina. Using his education as a tool, for he had traveled widely and spoke many languages, Vesey, in 1822, carefully laid the plans for an uprising intended to motivate masses of slaves to revolt.[5] Although their attempt was crushed, there were to be others in other years and at other places led by Negroes who had gained some rudiments of education.

Among slaves there are the examples of Gabriel Prosser, who in 1800 organized over a thousand slaves outside Richmond, Virginia, and Nat Turner, a literate preacher of recognized intelligence who drew illustrations from the Bible to give impetus to the act of rebelling against injustice. Although he did not, like Vesey, work out an elaborate plan, Turner used the scriptures to embolden his followers in the bloody massacre of 1831. As for the uncountable slave revolts that did occur sporadically throughout the South, most were entirely without any theoretical foundation, a deficiency which could, at least in part, account for their consistent failure. Education never reached the masses of southern slaves and those who rose to lead them—whether slave or free—lacked any opportunity for meeting with and rallying to their side a large assemblage. If freedom was to be achieved, it was for the most part through the tried and true practice of direct escape, for which no theoretical preparation was required.

After the revolts of Gabriel, Vesey, and Turner, educational facilities for free blacks were suppressed. Schools were closed, and the legal arm of southern society further exerted its control over blacks' existence. So serious was the threat in the minds of southern slaveholders of free blacks rousing slaves to rebel that efforts were made to have them removed from the plantation area and restrictions placed on their freedom of movement.

Outside inspiration for revolt was confined to the black preachers who continued to give religious instruction on the plantations, the more sophisticated of them citing the example of the Jews' escape from Egypt to motivate their congregations to flee their bondage,[6] and pointing to passages in scripture which "proved" the equality of the races. Increasingly, the act of escape drew from the Bible for its sanction. Harriet Tubman and Sojourner Truth—two major organizers of the underground railroad—were apt to give encouragement to runaways by quoting from the scriptures and drawing vivid and hallowed precedents from the stories in the Bible. By force of analogy and appeal to universal human emotions, Bible instruction, up until the time of the Civil War, was the major source of subversive resistance to the slaveocracy.

In the North the situation was otherwise. The greater opportunity for a wider education and the theoretical foundations laid by the white abolitionists, who began attacking slavery on philosophical and moral grounds, did much to instruct the black masses of the North. One of the most formidable undertakings of the abolitionists was a full-scale defense of Negro equality. Through books, newspapers, and on the lecture platform the abolitionists, Negro and white, defended the equality of the Negro and set out to convince the American public that the Negro was not only entitled to freedom, but that he could contribute to American life and democracy. Although the abolitionists were a tiny minority, through their persistence they helped forge the attitudes that ended slavery, enfranchised the Negro, and gave him citizenship. In the final analysis, argued abolitionists, the question was not one of race, but of human rights.

Both Negro and white abolitionists suffered from internal dissension over fundamental questions of policy and ideology. By the end of the 1840s the appeals of the most radical arguments were gaining support in Negro conventions, newspapers, and antislavery tracts. Even Frederick Douglass abandoned his previous conviction that moral persuasion and nonresistance alone could abolish slavery. Still more extreme members of the black community denied the efficacy of assimilation and integration as a solution to the problems facing them in America—nothing short of the creation of an independent black nation could ensure the conditions of life and culture whereby blacks could reach their full self-development. Such were the arguments of Martin Robinson Delany writing in 1852, considered to be the "father" of black nationalism.[7]

With the spur to ideological formulation gained through the abolitionist movement, there occurred in the decades before the Civil War increased acts of individual and organized revolt through the underground railroads, along with a mounting appeal to the laws of the land. Certainly in the North there was by this time no lack of ideas in the search for a solution to the black man's burden in America, any more than there was common agreement as to which solutions once put into practice would be most likely to end the conditions of slavery. If black history has a common core, it can be found in the persistent search for the techniques necessary to win the struggle for freedom and equality in this country. Depending both upon individual personalities and the changing context and climate of American life, black thought has been alternately simplistic, mythic, utopian, religious and otherworldly; as well as complex, rational, pragmatic, benevolent, and vengeful: above all, it has had to be adaptive, creative, dynamic, and bold. Anyone wishing to appreciate the spectrum of black social and political thinking must first recognize the enormously complex emotional forces at play in this never-ending struggle to be truly free men.

The main preoccupation of black thought, up until the Emancipation Proclamation, was simply freedom. After the Civil War, with freedom nominally won, attention was centered on the issue of Negro suffrage. With the passage of the Fifteenth Amendment it seemed to most blacks that their long-hoped for entry into full citizenship was at hand. During the reconstruction period black intellectual thought subsided as Negroes for the first time began to involve themselves in the business of politics and earning a living.

With freedom seemingly so close, the forces working to undo the achievements of reconstruction were barely heeded. But with the withdrawal of all federal troops from the South after the disputed national election of 1876, and the forces that restrained racism visibly weakened, the light of freedom receded. Throughout the South the whites recaptured their former position of power and quickly saw to it that all the means at their disposal were employed to maintain their authority.

First, the blacks were disenfranchised from their brief taste of political participation in the South.[8] Next, the rise of Jim Crow statutes attempted to permanently fix the black man in a subservient role in American society, substantiated by the self-justifying ideologies of social Darwinism and racism based on the presumption of the innate inferiority of blacks. The often subtle, disguised, and uneven fashion in which these ideas found expression made it difficult for black thinkers to react in a concerted way; that is, until the problems intensified to a degree that action of any kind was demanded.

The reactions to the renewed hostilities of discrimination and segregation were diverse and extreme. One "Pap" Singleton led an exodus of Negroes westward in 1879, in search of a place where blacks could at least find peace, security, and liberty.[9] Others, following the example of Singleton, found several northern communities. Advocates of a return to Africa, whose chief exponent was H. M. Turner, the militant leader of black reconstruction in Georgia, were motivated by the conviction that the blacks could never achieve manhood in the United States. Counter to these radical flights of a tiny minority, the mood for the majority of blacks was one of sullen acquiescence.

When, in 1895, Booker T. Washington spoke at the Atlanta Cotton Exposition, it marked a new point of departure in the currents of black thought. Washington sought an accommodation to segregation and discrimination through the puritan values of self-help, hard work, and discipline. He suggested a program of industrial education for blacks, which, if sincerely pursued, would bring economic security and the respect of the white community. With the requisite training Negroes could compete in the industrial marketplace; they could

establish their own businesses and gradually develop
their own communities.[10] The assumption underlying
this path to progress was that by imitating the standards
and values of the white community racial prejudice
would automatically disappear; that with economic respectability would come black political equality.

While the migration of southern Negroes to the
northern cities grew in the 1890s, the accommodation
advocated by Washington drew the support not only of
Negroes seeking new economic opportunities but of
white leaders and philanthropists who directly sought
his advice. However, the changing conditions of Negro
life in the first decades of the twentieth century—their
numerical strength and their right to vote in the northern cities, both potentially powerful political weapons
—acted to diminish Washington's influence in favor of
more uncompromising statements of the Negro position.
Here Monroe Trotter, W. A. Fortune, and W. E. B.
Du Bois led the way to a more radical attack on the
problem of political rights. Two major black organizations—the National Afro-American League and the
Niagara Association—were formed with the purpose of
protesting for civil rights within the framework of the
Constitution. These gave way to the NAACP which
proposed education, legal action, and organization to
fight the discrimination hindering the free development
of Negro individuals. The Association assumed that
when Americans knew of injustice, their intelligence
and moral principles would demand reform from legislatures and courts.

The first answer given by Du Bois to the problems
of blacks lay in what he called the "talented tenth." If
one-tenth of the black elite were to focus their special

training, insights, and ability on the problems of the masses of black people, techniques and methods would be found to raise them from their misery. Shortly after enunciating this idea, Du Bois joined the NAACP, giving its program his full assent. In the progressivism of the Association he saw the chance of freeing the Negro from concentration on his own progress and uniting him with the larger cause of world uplift. After the Paris Peace Conference in 1919, which Du Bois attended for the purpose of gaining if not a place at least recognition for the black colonials in the League of Nations, he embraced a Pan-Africanism.[11] By internationalizing the race problem he hoped to create a more powerful agency for change. But, after the disappointing outcome of five Pan-African congresses, this hope was abandoned.

His ideas always changing, depending on how regional, national, or international developments affected the Negro people, Du Bois could be found advocating moderation or retaliatory violence, integration or separatism, Pan-Africanism or anti-Garveyism, reform or radicalism, anti-Communism or Communism, elitism or proletarian involvement. These shifts in posture reflected not uncertainty as to goals, but rather the constant need to reassess a theoretical position in the light of empirical losses and gains. Integration and racial solidarity were the two seemingly conflictful ideas that remained constant themes in Du Bois' writing, ideas that have persisted at the center of black debate.

Whereas both Washington and Du Bois had failed to reach the Negro masses, to express their aspirations and mirror their discontents, Marcus Garvey and his Universal Negro Improvement Association caught the imagination of hundreds of thousands of Negroes who joined it. With its program of black nationalism, "back to Africa," and Negro economic independence, the UNIA became the first mass movement among Negroes in the United States. Garvey's message of race solidarity and pride was appropriately timed for an audience deeply frustrated in their pursuit of the American promise in the period immediately following World War I. Coming at a time when Negroes generally had so little of which to be proud, Garvey's appeal to race pride and his vision of a great independent African nation where Negroes could achieve their destiny as a great people, stirred a powerful response in the hearts of his black listeners.

Convinced that Negroes could expect no permanent progress in a land dominated by white men, and concerned lest the Negro should forget his racial and cultural background, Garvey willingly relinquished Negro rights in America for the dubious right to establish a black nation in Africa. Although Garvey's scheme to resettle black Americans in Africa had, by 1924, ended in financial disaster, his belief that freedom, independence, and self-respect could never be achieved by the Negro in America has continued to find confirmation by black nationalists of a later era.

The utopian dream of an escape from America to some nether shore where black people would fully come into their own did not die with the miscarriage of Garvey's African plan. It appeared, transformed, in the preaching of Father Divine and Daddy Grace,[12] self-styled "divine" prophets, who created for the confused, bewildered, and despairing black masses of the thirties an idyllic vision of a heavenly home where none of the misery of this world exists, and which could be entered by all—for a fee. For a while, the black masses saw the answer to all their worldly problems in this fantasy of another realm, a black heaven, where the reward for all their sufferings awaited. Through religious salvation— available through the paid guidance of these self-appointed prophets—lay the road to freedom and equality.

During the depression years, belief in utopian solutions to black problems reached the pinnacle of fantasized wish-fulfillment. The naive credulity of the black masses had been stretched as far as it could, when the situation desperately called for concrete action, tangible relief. This time the lead came from the federal government. The social welfarism of the New Deal taught blacks that changes affecting the quality of their daily lives could emanate from as remote an instrument as the central governing authority. It also taught them, through the example of union leaders like Walter Reuther, that the government could be prodded into action by means of demonstrations, mass protests, sit-ins, picketing, strikes, and slow-downs. Through techniques of direct action, the government and employers could be made to change practices or policies held by the majority to be undesirable.

Thousands of miles from America, another use of direct action protest was being successfully employed by Mahatma Gandhi against the British in India. Back home, a group of army veterans organized a march on Washington and, in an unprecedented act, camped on the White House lawn in the hope of influencing a change in presidential policy.[13] In the forties, direct action was employed by the Fellowship of Reconciliation, a pacifist organization, against armament manufacturers in an effort to stop the production of war materials. While not each employment of the direct action technique resulted in having all the demands of the protestors met, their successes were remarkable enough for the method to be picked up by leaders of the black community. Adam Clayton Powell employed boycotts, sit-ins, protests, and marches to help the members of his church in Harlem secure jobs, better pay, and better positions.[14] After the attack on Pearl Harbor, the FOR again used these techniques to attack discrimination and segregation in restaurants in Chicago's Loop area.[15]

The question in the minds of the black community was now one of how far such methods could be used to combat segregation and discrimination, and whether direct action should include violent as well as nonviolent means. This raised further questions as to the probable reaction and ultimate effect on Negro goals of each and every form of direct protest. There were black leaders who were impressed with the simplicity and effectiveness of Reuther's techniques—a form of pressure that remained peaceful until provoked. Gandhi's method, on the other hand, had behind it a fully elaborated doctrine: it was as much a theory as it was a practice. Whether direct action could in all cases work as effectively without a doctrine to substantiate each of its gestures is a question that remains with us today.

The split that occurred in black leadership circles, however, was not over whether it was advisable to embrace a full-blown theory of direct action, but over the issue of violence versus nonviolence. To study the subject at firsthand, blacks journeyed to India to discuss with Gandhi the application of his technique and the feasibility of its use by black Americans. In 1929, a group of blacks led by Mordecai Johnson heard Gandhi tell them that not only was his technique suitable, but that "perhaps it will be through the Negro that the unadulterated message of nonviolence will be delivered to the world." Successive groups of blacks, led by Protestant ministers Howard Thurman, Benjamin Mays, and Channing Tobias, visited Gandhi in the thirties to discuss the same question, and received from him the same encouragement.

Corroborating Gandhi's belief that nonviolence would prove an effective tactic for blacks in America was the prominent white theologian, Reinhold Niebuhr, who felt that this was the very means needed to extricate blacks from their lowly position in the American caste system.[16] It also seemed to Niebuhr in keeping with black religious traditions because it combined the aggressiveness of young blacks with the patient forbearance of their elders. Niebuhr's reasoning was particularly convincing to those black theologians interested in pursuing the path of nonviolence.

Other black leaders, some ministers among them, held to the view that they were a powerless minority controlled by a powerful majority, and doubted the effectiveness of nonviolence. Although the preponderance of black leaders throughout the twenties and thirties were ministers, there were those among them who did not accept the Christian foundation on which the theory of nonviolence rested. The debate, which had raged back and forth, was clearly set forth in a symposium which appeared in *Crisis,* the journal of the NAACP, in 1924.[17] Black minister James Weldon Johnson, while condemning physical force, did not accept nonviolent direct action as the final tool for black emancipation. E. Franklin Frazier, the black sociologist, followed the same line of thinking when he stated that nonviolence would become just another form of self-abasement for blacks. Nor did he hesitate to reveal his contempt for the redemptive power of love. Self-respect, he felt, was much more important for blacks than the soul-saving power attributed to nonviolence.[18]

While the pros and cons of the relevancy and efficacy of nonviolent direct action continued to be debated in the thirties, leaders such as Adam Clayton Powell, Jr. employed it on purely pragmatic grounds, denying the powers of moral suasion based on Christian love others attributed to it. Powell upheld nonviolence as a potent, energetic tool, believing that violence itself was, in the end, self-defeating.

In the forties, the black labor leader, Asa Philip Randolph, called for a black nonviolent mass march on Washington to protest the exclusion of blacks from employment in the production boom generated by the outbreak of the Second World War. Many holders of defense contracts were in the habit of employing Negroes for only the most menial jobs, despite a state of national emergency which called for all the hands available to join in the war effort. Randolph planned to model his march on Washington after the famous Bonus March of 1932.[19] His popularity within the black community and his proven organizational skills—he had only four years earlier broken a company union and organized the sleeping-car porters—made his threatened march something to reckon with. Several conferences with President Roosevelt failed to deter Randolph from his stated purpose and forced the President to issue his now famous executive order outlawing job discrimination in defense industries. The intended march on Washington won its point on strictly pragmatic grounds; recourse to Gandhian moral arguments were not necessary.

The use of nonviolence to alter the structure of race relations was brought into use around the same time by two young blacks, James Farmer and Bayard Rustin, who had been hired by FOR (Fellowship of Reconciliation) in 1941. Rustin conducted one-man campaigns consisting mostly of sit-ins at segregated restaurants, while Farmer turned his attention to creating a national organization devoted to combating segregation through nonviolent direct action. In Chicago, in 1942, the FOR regional youth secretary, George Houser, began conducting interracial sit-ins at an exclusive, segregated restaurant. Eventually, aided by the sympathetic reaction of customers who began asking those determined to be served to join them at their tables, all of the group were seated, and, for the first time, segregation in a northern restaurant was ended by persistent but nonviolent means.

Finally, in 1943, the Chicago committee on racial equality and the FOR national organization joined in forming the Congress of Racial Equality (CORE), choosing as its chairman James Farmer. From 1943 to 1955, leadership in applying nonviolent techniques to race relations came from the numerous CORE chapters across the country. They staged restaurant sit-ins, theater stand-ins, business boycotts, and bought stock in segregated corporations in order to launch complaints at shareholders' meetings. In one instance, in State College, Pennsylvania, CORE, unable to persuade the town's barbers to serve Negroes, financed a new barber shop that would serve patrons without regard to race.

CORE and FOR combined forces to conduct the first "freedom ride" in 1946, out of which grew the first case to test the constitutionality of segregated seating on state buses *(Morgan v. Virginia)*. Deliberately ignoring the Supreme Court's ruling that this constituted a violation of the constitutional guarantee of freedom of interstate commerce, the southern bus companies, under pressure from state officials, did virtually nothing to alter their old practice. To challenge the implementation of the Morgan decision, a bus journey by an interracial group through the upper South, called the Journey of Reconciliation, was planned by the two organizations. Those actively participating received intensive training in nonviolence techniques before their departure and NAACP attorneys stood by to give legal aid. On the whole, however, CORE's attacks on segregation and discrimination remained piecemeal, unsystematic, and relatively uncoordinated; directed mainly at the upper South rather than the deep South. Increasingly, by the 1960s, CORE came to rely less and less on moral grounds and more on political expediency.[20]

While CORE, Powell, and Randolph were practicing nonviolent direct action without special call to moral persuasion, other black intellectuals and religious leaders were building its moral foundations and examining the expanded possibilities to be gained by stressing the redemptive power of love and the example of Christ.

Howard Thurman, an outstanding black theologian, in his book *Jesus and the Disinherited,* attempted to establish the rudiments of a moral theory for nonviolent political action by arguing that every man is potentially every other man's neighbor and "a man must love his neighbor directly, clearly permitting no barriers between." According to Thurman, the religion of Jesus states that the disinherited has the obligation to "love his enemy" because the artificial racial barrier constructed to divide men into different groups denies them the awareness of their common humanity, which, through love, could be restored. Love, Thurman felt, could transform the social order.

Following Thurman, Mordecai Johnson, then president of Howard University, became the chief spokesman for the idea that the moral power of nonviolent action could change race relations. The power of love could not, he felt, be excelled either for bringing about improvement in the social order or for cementing its breaches. But, despite the fine theoretical structure of Thurman's appeal and the continued exhortations of Johnson, arguments for the morality of nonviolence bypassed the black masses. Both men remained the expounders of an idea, but not its practitioners. In fact, during the forties, no other nonviolent direct actions were organized apart from those of CORE and a proposed action to defy the draft called by A. Philip Randolph and Grant Reynolds in 1947. And even this was publicly called off when President Truman, in 1948, issued an executive order banning segregation in the armed forces.[21]

Similarly, there were few campaigns involving nonviolent direct action in the early fifties. In the years following the Korean conflict, the United States sank into a period of citizen silence. What had begun as attacks on organizations working for social change became attacks on any individual who raised his voice on a controversial subject or was suspected of holding ideas or attitudes that were "different." These repressive attacks became institutionalized through the House Un-American Activities Committee, and later in the Senate through a similar committee headed by Senator James Eastland of Mississippi, and most flamboyantly through the work of Senator Joseph McCarthy. By the mid-fifties, American citizens, both black and white, had stopped going to meetings, joining organizations, or even signing petitions. McCarthyism and the emergence of the "silent generation" combined to make social protest of any kind unpopular and even dangerous.

Then on 1 December 1955, Mrs. Rosa Parks was arrested in Montgomery, Alabama for refusing to give up her seat on a city bus to a white passenger. Her arrest set off the Montgomery bus boycott, which was then led to a spectacularly successful conclusion by the twenty-six-year-old Reverend Doctor Martin Luther King, Jr. This sparked the beginning of a new outlook and theoretical construction which was to characterize the black struggle for social justice and equality throughout the fifties and sixties until the emergence of the more militant black power movement.

King became the proponent of nonviolent direct action chiefly because he saw in it a great moral force. Like black leaders before him, he constructed his own theoretical explanation to underpin and justify the black revolution underway from many quarters in the sixties. Unlike many former black leaders, King, like Gandhi, was an activist as well; also, like Gandhi, he was an organizer able to reconcile disparate factions. He established the Southern Christian Leadership Conference in 1957 to coordinate the work of direct action groups that had sprung up in southern cities. Like other black theologians, he possessed the additional strength of oratory, of being able to make his ideas known, convincing, and accepted. He embodied the qualities of the leader as well as the dreamer, the protagonist at the dramatic center of a historic struggle for human rights, and the thoughtful philosopher concerned with the ultimate questions of human nature and destiny. It is not, however, with an evaluation of King's political actions that we are presently concerned, but with his moral and political philosophy as it affected and motivated his actions.

Prior to any understanding of King's philosophy, it is important to know the role he accorded black people in history. In his view, blacks had a mission to fulfill beyond their struggle for justice and equality, namely, the introduction of a new moral standard in American life. Although the idea of a specific black mission did not originate with King, he drew from and enlarged upon the already existing belief in the redemption of white American society through the Christ-like suffering and love of its black outcasts.

The notion that the black man had a unique function to fulfill in the American culture began to appear in the latter part of the nineteenth century. The earliest arguments stated that the ultimate purpose of black people in this world would be expressed in their carrying out God's divine plan. With the emergence of a better educated black clergy at the turn of the century, the task of reforming society was transferred from God's hands to the black man's;[22] but the mission remained the same. Several black intellectuals, such as W. E. B. Du Bois and E. Franklin Frazier, elaborated or modified the reasons or the means for the mission's being performed, but they basically concurred in accepting the ideology of a black messianic redemption of the sins of American society. Fresh interpretations which sought to give credence to this role were made by black writers and artists such as Jean Toomer, Countée Cullen, Langston Hughes, and Nella Larsen, but these too failed to challenge the basic premise.

Along with the special mission ideology there had also developed a particular image of the Negro. Many blacks, because of their patience, humility, and good-natured forbearance, conceived of themselves as Christ-like. These self-concepts were, however, rationalizations born out of conditions of slavery; ego defense mechanisms contrived to maintain self-respect during a time when the choice in handling aggression was either to repress it or to be destroyed by it.

After the abolition of slavery these subservient traits became elevated to the status of virtuous behavior and moral superiority. It became possible to look down on one's white counterparts as morally inferior, possibly inhuman, and certainly lacking in Christian grace. It was in imitation of the image of Christ that the Negro subculture elevated itself to a new measure of self-esteem. Psychologically, this was not a new phenomenon, for, as Bertrand Russell noted: "All movements in behalf of oppressed groups have found it necessary to claim moral superiority for their constituents in order to justify their having the same right as everybody else."[23] From feelings of moral righteousness grew the belief in a special saving mission for blacks to perform, an obligation to rejuvenate and spiritualize America.

King not only accepted the black mythology of a saving Christ, he made it the cornerstone of his political philosophy. It was the mission of the black man to teach the white man the capacity to love.[24] The white man's sickness, as King perceived it, stemmed from his need for ego-gratification, which led to the pursuit of material things and status; which in turn caused man's alienation from his fellowmen and dehumanization.

Under the conditions of slavery, according to King, people became objects to one another and an "I"–"it" relationship was established. Since such a relationship precludes a sense of community and brotherhood, it must first be converted to an "I"–"thou" relationship whereby true community could be restored and depersonalization disappear. To achieve this sense of community, King argued that blacks had to suffer creatively for whites; through their suffering and redemptive love, humaneness would be restored to the social order. Thus, in King's thought, the cardinal role of blacks in American society was to infuse a sense of love, thereby decreasing the power of materialism and opening the way for the emergence of the "beloved community." Furthermore, King saw in this divine plan how the existence of evil could be accounted for, including that committed by white Americans, and how black Americans could be instrumental in undoing this evil.[25]

Nonviolent action readily lent itself, in King's mind, to a fulfillment of the black mission within the limits and standards set by the example of Christ. In King's hands, nonviolence became an end in itself, endowed with superior moral qualities which, eventually, were to bring about a reconstituted society. By calling upon the best Christian virtues of blacks and exhorting them to desist from the temptation of violence, King asked them to believe that their highest destiny—to redeem America from the curse of racism—would be gloriously won. Nor would the example of black righteousness be confined to stirring the conscience of America alone. Upon receipt of the Nobel Peace Prize, King stated that the black nonviolent struggle for equality could be symbolic to other groups and nations as well. It might even be possible for the Negro, through adherence to nonviolence, "to challenge the nations of the world so that they will seriously seek an alternative to war and destruction."[26]

One must, in examining King's philosophy, bear in mind the relationship between the black's mission, the role this bound him to in American society, and the purifying technique which, by absolving the world of its evil, would bring about a new era. The method of nonviolence, its merits, attributes, strengths and weaknesses, are all carefully assessed by King in his writing, speeches, and interviews; however, he is less clear about the end product, the beloved community. Yet, whatever lack of definition his vision may have suffered from, the beloved community was decidedly an integrated one, representative of an idealized future where all men live as brothers and equals in justice and harmony.

The integration of all races and classes of men was King's constant, overriding goal and the only answer he saw to the black man's problems in America. His critics, chief among them the new advocates of black power, disagreed to both his ends and means. Black power advocates have argued that violence is as just, possessed of as many soul-saving qualities as nonviolence. And they have challenged racial integration as an end in itself. The position originally advanced by Stokely Carmichael, calling for a self-determined separatism and arguing that since the white man has failed to solve the problems of the black community in over three hundred years, he could hardly be expected to do so now, echoes the vehement separatism of Marcus Garvey. Carmichael's emphasis on the greatest possible reliance on self-help is reminiscent of Booker T. Washington urging black economic independence. Integration, claim the separatists, diminishes black culture and proper racial pride, besides hindering the natural good nature of blacks from fully asserting itself.

The debate between the integrationists and the black nationalists continues to draw new fuel and fire, with black people aligning to whichever side most suits their

outlook. At the moment, a radical black power movement is the latest expression of the black man's struggle
for freedom and social justice in America. But there
will be other, equally radical expressions and explorations of the ways to that end, so long as it is not attained.

Until very recently, the Negro rarely set up separate
cultural values or developed divergent institutional loyalties or political objectives. Negro ideologies have in
the past tended to remain inside democratic institutions
and traditions. Martin Luther King, Jr.'s example is
primarily that of a revolutionary struggle to elevate the
spirit of the black man, improve his material condition,
and reach for a world of Christian harmony here on
earth; all within the limits of the democratic process.
Out of the cumulative emotional, spiritual, political,
and human needs of black people was the particular
amalgam of King's philosophy wrought.

NOTES

1. Schlesinger, *A Thousand Days,* pp. 976–977.
2. Jenkins, *Pro-Slavery Thought in the Old South*, pp. 240–
86; Newby, *Development of Segregationist Thought.*
3. For information on this point, see Carter G. Woodson,
The Education of the Negro Prior to 1861 (New York: G. P.
Putnam's Sons, 1915), and E. Horace Fitchett, "The Traditions of
the Free Negroes in Charleston, South Carolina," *Journal of
Negro History* (April 1940), pp. 139–52.
4. For instance, blacks in Virginia sent the legislature a petition in 1675, while those in North Carolina as early as 1726, and
in South Carolina in 1791. For additional information see Aptheker, *A Documentary History of the Negro People.*
5. According to E. Franklin Frazier, Vesey was acquainted
with the successful uprisings of slaves in Haiti and used the
Haitian uprising to encourage his own followers in their planned
revolt. Frazier further states that: "he also had some knowledge

of the principles of the French Revolution and was aware of the debates in Congress on the Missouri Compromise. Having such a knowledge he used every occasion to instill in the Negroes confidence and a sense of their equality with whites," in *Negro in the United States,* p. 88.

6. Delany, writing in 1852, stated that although blacks in America were separated in terms of distance and locale as well as status (slave and free) from each other, they nevertheless represented "a nation within a nation as (did) the Poles in Russia, (and) the Hungarians in Austria." Black people, he argued, "have native hearts and virtues, just as other nations, which in their pristine purity are noble, potent, and worthy of example." Delany suggested that the elevation of black people could be accomplished by their migrating to another country, and he made several trips to Africa to inquire into the possibility of establishing a black nation. America, as he saw it, was bad for blacks because the system instituted by whites would never permit full black self-development. Although Delany's theory only attracted nominal support, his proposition and thesis linger in black political thought.

7. Botkin, ed., *Lay My Burden Down,* p. 82.

8. See *Origins of the New South 1877–1913* (Baton Rouge, La.: State University Press, 1967), pp. 321–29.

9. Fleming, " 'Pap' Singleton, Moses of the Colored Exodus," and Garvin, "Benjamin or 'Pap' Singleton and His Followers."

10. Meier, *Negro Thought in America,* pp. 42–59.

11. Rayford Logan, "The Historical Aspects of Pan-Africanism, 1900–1945," in *Pan-Africanism Reconsidered,* edited by the American Society of African Culture (Berkeley: University of California Press, 1962).

12. Bontemps and Conroy, *Anyplace But Here,* pp. 19–76.

13. John D. Hicks et al., *The American Nation* (Boston: Houghton Mifflin Co., 1963), p. 39.

14. Powell, *Marching Blacks.*

15. Peck, *Freedom Rides.*

16. Niebuhr, *Moral Man and Immoral Society,* pp. 251–54.

17. Bennett, *What Manner of Man,* p. 73.

18. Ibid.

19. Hicks et al., *American Nation,* p. 151.

20. Bell, *CORE and the Strategy of Nonviolence,* p. 36.

21. Logan, *The Negro in the United States,* pp. 159–61.

22. Fullinwider, *The Mind and Mood of Black America,* p. 93.

23. Bertrand Russell, "The Superior Virtue of the Oppressed," *Unpopular Essays* (New York: Simon and Schuster, 1950), pp. 58–64. See also James W. Vander Zanden, *Race Relations in Transition: The Segregation in the South* (New York: Random House, 1964).

24. Fullinwider, op. cit., pp. 235–38.

25. Ibid.

26. King, "The Nobel Prize."

3 | *The Foundation of King's Moral and Political Philosophy*

Negro thinking in social and political terms is thus exclusively a thinking about the Negro problem.

The Negro leader, the Negro social scientist, the Negro man of art and letters is disposed to view all social, economic, political, indeed esthetic and philosophic issues from the Negro angle.

Negro thinking is thinking under the pressure and conflicts to which the Negro is subjected.[1]

POLITICAL philosophy, because it touches upon the whole of man's condition, cannot be content to address itself solely to practical political questions. Nor are mere opinion and belief sufficient to provide answers to the great social and political issues, which require the resources of every area of knowledge, plus imagination, flexibility, and reason. The public life of Martin Luther King, Jr. is illustrative of the evolution of a political philosophy—if we define philosophy as the culmination of the passion for justice—and the search for more deeply integrated principles with which to guide political conduct.

That which we call political theory, on the other hand, need not comprise an entire political system, but may deal with a facet of political life, set forth a particular policy, a general principle, or a set of empirical generalizations. But, whether of a more empiric or philosophical character, whether a partial or complete system, common to all political thought are certain moral assumptions, factual and descriptive material, and generalizations with which to order the masses of political phenomena and the complications of policy making.[2] Even the most modest attempts at theory building, which pass as political "ideas" either contain or imply the foregoing elements and present some type of case for government.

Underlying each type of political system is a more or less cohesive body of principles according to which it operates, and a body of normative beliefs with which it justifies its actions. Carried to its logical extension then, any political idea may be said to explain and justify a political system. Broadly speaking, political systems may be classified and studied according to their method of treating political conflict and the policies to which a government is bound.

In the sense that King's political philosophy offers no alternative to the present American system of government, it is incomplete. Like most partial political theories, he emphasizes some elements at the expense of others, and, in the main, it is prescriptive, given to recommedations for change within the existing system. Nonviolent civil disobedience is the primary and necessary means of effecting social and political change. Whether or not his political thought was comprehensive enough to earn him the title of political philosopher, in the strictest sense, his concepts of the best political system, the nature and limits of political obligation, and the ethical premises of peaceful change, are valuable in themselves and deserve careful assessment.

Three questions that can be found at the center of

all political thought, and to which King addressed himself, are the nature and functions of man, his relation to the rest of the universe—which involves a consideration of the meaning of life as a whole—and, emerging from the interaction of these two, the problem of the relation of each man to his fellow men. The latter, the main concern of political theory in its narrowest sense, involves a discussion of the nature, purpose, and functions of the state. Man, his ultimate goal in life, his social activities, all are constantly interacting, creating from their contact the web of material which political thinkers and statesmen attempt to disentangle, organize, and manipulate.

According to their method of approaching their subject, political thinkers are generally classified as either idealists or pragmatists, employing deductive or inductive reasoning respectively, though both forms of inquiry may, and frequently do, overlap in the same thinker. King's, as we shall see, was primarily a deductive mind, proceeding from moral speculations on the nature of man, his proper condition on earth, and his purpose in life, to finding a tangible means in organized public action which would give his world view practical political focus. But his speculations on the nature of man had themselves grown out of the stuff of daily observation and awareness, from the feelings and reactions of his early life, i.e., by induction.

OF INFLUENCES AND THE INFLUENTIAL

In his youth King became acutely aware of the economic and racial injustice, of the evil, within society, and felt compelled to seek a means of rectifying these conditions. He stated that he had grown up abhoring segregation and the oppressive, barbarous, and brutal acts it engendered. "I have passed spots where Negroes had been savagely lynched and had watched the Ku Klux Klan on its rides at night. I had seen police brutality with my own eyes and watched Negroes receive the most tragic injustices in the courts."[3] Such incidences as well as the continuing harshness of the segregation system led King to begin a serious intellectual quest for a way to eliminate the results if not the source of racism in American society.

Although, owing to his family's economic comfort, King himself escaped much of the harshness of racial injustice, he could not remove from his mind the economic insecurity of his playmates and the "tragic poverty" which engulfed the Auburn Avenue Ghetto in Atlanta, Georgia, where he grew up. Working, as a teenager, he became even more conscious of the oppressive nature of segregation. Employed in a plant that hired both blacks and whites, he saw the "economic injustices firsthand, and realized that the poor white was exploited just as much as the Negro." Successive childhood experiences made him deeply conscious of the varieties of injustice in our society, and, as he pondered the possibilities of a career, concern with the condition of black people and their suffering was paramount. Until he was certain of the kind of occupation which would do the most good for his people, he could not commit himself to any.[4]

During his college years he came into contact with Thoreau's *Essay on Civil Disobedience* and was fascinated by the possibility of refusing to cooperate with an evil system. "I was so deeply moved that I reread the work several times. This was my first intellectual contact with the theory of nonviolence and resistance."[5] Later, in the seminary, he was to spend time studying the great social philosophers: Plato, Aristotle, Rousseau, Hobbes, Bentham, Mill, and Locke. Naturally, he learned a great deal from these, but it was Walter Rauschenbush's *Christianity and the Social Crisis* that provided theological basis for his own social concern. In his view, Rauschenbush's significance was in his insistance upon the gospel being attuned to the "whole man" —his body and his soul—his material as well as his spiritual wellbeing. In reading Rauschenbush, King realized that in order for Christianity to be relevant to man— be he black or white—it had to deal with not only the spiritual realm but with man's everyday socioeconomic environment. Any religion that did not concern itself with both realms of human existence was a religion of little merit and out of touch with reality.[6]

While taking his theological degree at Crozier Theological Seminary, King was still dubious about the power of love to solve social problems. "The 'turn the other cheek' philosophy and the 'love your enemies' philosophy are only valid, I felt, when individuals are in conflict with other individuals; when racial groups and nations are in conflict, a more realistic approach is necessary."[7] Then one Sunday afternoon, King traveled to Philadelphia to hear a sermon by Dr. Mordecai Johnson. Dr. Johnson spoke on the life and teaching of Mahatma Gandhi. Gandhi's message had an immediate and profound impact upon King and it was in reading the work of Gandhi that he lost his skepticism of the power of love and began to appreciate its usefulness and potency in the area of social reform.

It was the Gandhian concept of Satyagraha (satya is truth which equals love, and graha is force: satyagraha thus means truth-force or love-force) that had the strongest influence upon King, although, at this point, he had no clear notion as to how it might effectively be applied.[8] King felt that Gandhi was "the first person in history to lift the love ethic of Jesus above mere interaction between individuals." The Gandhian technique of love and nonviolence gave him a potent instrument for social and collective transformation which blacks could be taught to use in their struggle against oppression and injustice.

It was this method, according to King, which gave him the intellectual and moral satisfaction that he had missed in the "utilitarianism of Bentham and Mill, the revolutionary methods of Marx and Lenin, the social contract theory of Hobbes, the 'back to nature' optimism of Rousseau, and the superman philosophy of Nietzsche."[9] Cognizant now of a meaningful method, King yet was missing the kind of event in which it could be appropriately used. When, in 1955, the Montgomery bus boycott was organized and King, then twenty-six years old, accepted the responsibility of leadership, he was prepared to present to the people a fully articulated rationale and guidance following the ideal of Christ's Sermon on the Mount, and a technique which would become known as the Gandhian method.[10]

The next major influence on the development of King's social and political thought was Reinhold Niebuhr. Niebuhr, King felt, had presented incisive insights into human behavior, especially the behavior of groups and nations; more than any other theologian, he understood the complexities of human motives as well as the relationship between morality and power. "His theology," King said, "is a persistent reminder of the reality of sin on every level of man's existence. . . .

Moreover, Niebuhr helped me to recognize the complexity of man's social involvement and the glowing reality of collective evil."[11]

Reading Hegel, and his concept of dialectic, also contributed to the structuring of King's political philosophy. "His contention that 'truth is the whole' led me to a philosophical method of rational coherence. His analysis of the dialectical process helped me to see that growth comes through struggle."[12] During his stay at the seminary, King also adopted the subjective posture of personalism as set forth by Martin Buber, a doctrine contending that we must look to personality for the meaning of the universe, and that not only man but God too is supremely personal. From this grew two convictions: "Personalism gave me metaphysical and philosophical grounding for the idea of a personal God, and it gave me a metaphysical basis for the dignity and worth of all human personality."[13]

By 1954, King's formal training had ended and he had merged these relatively divergent intellectual forces into a positive social philosophy. "One of the main tenets of this philosophy was the conviction that nonviolent resistance was one of the most potent weapons available to oppressed people in their quest for social justice."[14] From Jesus, Thoreau and Gandhi had come the philosophical roots for King's theory of nonviolent social change; from Christ's Sermon on the Mount, with its emphasis on humility, self-criticism, forgiveness, and the renunciation of material gain, came the initial inspiration for a nonviolent approach; Thoreau's example had taught the rightfulness of civil disobedience; and Gandhi showed that there was a method for mass nonviolent resistance to the state. As one author has put it:

The teachings of the Great Three—Jesus, Thoreau, and Gandhi have been brought together. . . . The new synthesis is known simply as a "philosophy of love." It is not just a theory; it is an alternative to the conflict and killing that we usually associate with social progress.[15]

The philosophy of love, as the theologian would call it, or this philosophy of social reform, as it would be seen by the sociologist, was expressed politically as nonviolent civil disobedience; the form in which the ideal of love might result in practical action without violation or contradiction of that ideal.

THE METAPHYSICAL BASES

King's political philosophy and the technique he approved for implementing social change were a direct outgrowth of his religious and moral principles, of his metaphysical stand. For King, political life without religious principles was a soul-destroying process; for politics, like other human activities, must be governed either by morality or immorality. Without the moral basis religion provides, life would be a mere maze of nothingness, a depersonalized and alien thing.[16] By religion, however, King understood not only Christianity but Judaism, Buddhism, and Mohammedanism as well. Nowhere does he define religion, but his writings are replete with considerations of the necessary and prime elements of a good religion. His is a dualistic view involving the metaphysical union of the human with the divine in a mutual relationship expressed through worship and love. A positive religion, in King's thought, grants man the inner stability with which to face life. It assures him of God's concern with his burdens and fears and places him within a universe that is worthy of his trust.[17]

Otherworldly as religion may seem to many, to King it descends from the loftiest heights to the lowest valleys. A true religion is necessarily concerned with man's social condition. It must deal at once with "both earth and heaven, both time and eternity"; it must operate on a vertical as well as a horizontal plane. By being active in both spheres, it is able to integrate men with God, men with men and "each man with himself." Otherwise, religion becomes an opiate of the people, non-nourishing, and totally irrelevant to the needs of mankind.[18] Because religion contains divine laws and precepts from which moral principles can be derived, it can determine standards for judgment. Without absolute standards of justice, King felt, one was left with an arbitrary ethical relativism, as in the communist system, which can only lead in a downward spiral to eventual destruction to all social and moral good. Under communism—as he perceived it—there exists "no divine government, no absolute moral order," and no fixed immutable principles. Consequently, "almost anything—force, violence, murder, lying—is a justifiable means to the 'millennial' end."[19] Relativism was an abhorrence to King since, in the absence of certain fixed principles, there could result every form of deceit and ultimate chaos.

Religion, therefore, was necessary to interpret the world in terms of man's godliness and to bridge the gap between what is and what ought to be. "Whereas science and politics give man knowledge which is power; religion gives man *wisdom* which is control. Politics and science deal mainly with facts; religion deals mainly with values. Whereas science and *politics* merely investigate; religion interprets. The two are not rivals. They are complementary. *Politics* and science keep religion from sinking into the valley of crippling irrationalism and paralyzing obscurantism. Religion prevents science and *politics* from falling into the marsh of obsolete materialism and moral nihilism."[20] Christianity—in contrast to the ethical relativism of communism—sets forth a system of absolute moral values that affirms God and certain immutable moral principles contained in the very structure of the universe. Belief in the God of Christianity necessarily implies absolutism and immutable moral precepts. Man, according to King, needs stable moral absolutes upon which to base standards of justice, and religion supplies this need. Right and wrong could not exist were they merely relative.

Since religion bids one to measure moral and spiritual progress against scientific and political progress, it provides divine sanction for ethical principles used to protest against injustice and social evil.[21] Christians, by their very commitment to the brotherhood of man and the fatherhood of God, are bound to share a passionate concern for social justice. They are also obliged, as Christians, to recognize world unity and repudiate such concepts as racism which erect barriers of color and caste. At the core of the Christian doctrine is a broad universalism which makes any segregation of mankind morally unjustifiable.[22]

Hence, in King's view, religion calls upon people to be of strong convictions, not of conformity; of moral belief, and not necessarily of social respectability; of unswerving ethical principles and not of relativism and efficiency. It commands one to live according to a higher loyalty.[23] Christians can never give supreme loyalty to any earth-bound idea or time-bound custom, because at the heart of the universe is the reality of God and the brotherhood of man, to which all Christians owe their first allegiance.[24]

Thus religion involves the whole of human life. It constitutes the entire gamut of man's activities, social, political, and economic, in one indivisible whole. From this it follows that political wrongs and unsuitable political institutions enormously hinder the realization of the greatest good. "If one is truly devoted to the religion of Jesus he will seek to rid the earth of social evils. The gospel is social as well as personal." The goal of life is, then, to stand up for truth and justice. In his words, "I still believe that standing up for the truth of God is the greatest thing in the world. This is the end of life. . . . The end of life is to do the will of God, come what may."[25] In order to achieve this goal, one must first unite himself with God and through this union the greatest good may come about: first the individual, then the group. Although man's moral pilgrimage has a destination beyond this earth, his constant striving will bring him closer and closer to the city of righteousness and the kingdom of God. The kingdom of God, while far from a present reality, could, King believes, exist in isolated instances of judgment, personal devotion, and some forms of group life.[26]

A living, unshakable faith in God was at the core of King's philosophy, a faith so strong that he let God guide him through situations of extreme crisis. Without such faith, he was of the opinion that the fullest life would never be attained and that one was not really competent to use nonviolence as a political technique. King's conception of God is that of perfect selfhood and infinite will. God performs miracles for man by bringing him closer to His law and in working out new creations through His law—and not in destroying the "laws of nature." "King is a theist, looking upon God not merely as an abstract force, as a deist would, but as a personality, though one not bound by body, time or space."[27]

King also believed that every human being, however degraded, has in him the divine spark, i.e., limitless potentiality for growth and the capacity for responding in a human way to kind, generous treatment.[28] For the soul of man partakes of the divine; it remains unconquered and unconquerable by even the mightiest forces. Therefore, only with a living faith in God can the technique of nonviolence be employed with complete confidence and to the greatest advantage. Without God, nonviolence is without substance and potency. Since God, for King, is life, goodness and all that it connotes is also God. This goodness of God cannot be fully perceived, appreciated, or modified.[29] Conceived of as apart from God, goodness becomes lifeless, existing only when it confers visible benefits. The same is true of morals: if they are to be part of us, morals must be considered and cultivated in relation to God. This reasoning led King to a strong belief in the existence of God as a supernatural being still working wonders in history, a creative force that levels evil and exalts justice. Religion strengthens the conviction that we are not alone in this vast and uncertain universe; it lets us know that a wise and loving God is with us "beneath and above the shifting sands of time."[30]

Man, therefore, is of a divine origin; cognizant, King believes, that "eternity is his ultimate habitat." Thus, he can never fully adjust to the demands of time nor can he permit the existence of evil in his midst: it must be driven from the "native soil of his soul before he can achieve moral and spiritual dignity." Nor, though he has the potential for both good and evil, can he pursue evil forever, for "conscience speaks to him and he is reminded of things divine."

Yet, the absence, negation, or dismissal of God from our common affairs gives rise to a feeling of helplessness and induces people to rely, instead, on violence. This sense of helplessness—due to lack of faith in God—also leads to feelings of inferiority, insecurity, jealousy, envy, and fear, which then lead to hate, and violence thrives on hate. Until "Hate multiplies hate, violence multiplies violence, and toughness multiplies toughness in a descending spiral of destruction."[31] The only way to avoid this destructive spiral is to put one's faith in God. Then one can walk through the dark night with the radiant conviction that all things conspire for good for those who love God. With faith in God, one can love, and love is the only force that can remove hate. Hatred and bitterness paralyze, confuse, and darken life, and create the serpent of fear. Love, on the other hand, releases life, harmonizes life, illumines life, and drives away fear.

Love, in King's view, "is the most durable power in the world." It is the highest good which man, over the centuries, has sought to discover. Love stands at the center of the cosmos. God is love, and he who loves participates in the being of God; just as he who hates does not know God. Hence, "we must love our enemies, because only by loving them can we know God and experience the beauty of His holiness."[32] In King's eyes, love transforms with redemptive power; it is moral, it creates and builds. "Hate," according to King, "scars the soul, distorts and divides the personality; whereas love, in an amazing and inexorable way unites it." Therefore, we can love every man because God loves him. King stressed that we are all potential sons of God, who through love, realize our potentiality.

Conscious of the innumerable definitions of God, because his manifestations were many, King defined him not only as a personal being above nature, forever giving meaning and direction to its processes, but also as an impersonal being in nature. For King, God was not only powerful and good, but austere, expressing his toughmindedness in his justice and his tenderheartedness in his love and grace.

In sum, God, for King, is the central truth of man. Firm faith in Him is indispensable for the good life, as well as for the effective employment of nonviolent resistance. All other allegiances and obligations are binding insofar as they are consistent with the basic loyalty we owe to God. Since God pervades the universe, there is no antithesis between God and man, and all apparently separate existences are unified in His transcendence. Man is not the servant of God, but possesses a free will. "Man is man because he is free to operate within the framework of his destiny." He is free to deliberate, to make decisions, and to choose between the alternatives of good and evil. It is this freedom which distinguishes him from the lower animals. However, while freedom is of the essence of man, it is not an absolute freedom, but one that always operates within the context of a predestined structure. He stated that:

> Freedom is always within the framework of destiny. But there is freedom. We are both free and destined. Freedom is the act of deliberating, deciding, and responding within our destined nature.[33]

Thus, King arrived at the position that "God permits evil in order to preserve the freedom of man, but he does not cause evil." Religion tells man that God does not will evil, because that which is willed is intended and the idea that God intended man to suffer diseases, sickness, and poverty is "sheer heresy"; a false picture of God as a devil rather than a loving father.[34] Evil exists, but it is the result of man's misuse of his freedom, not the creation of God. King saw the history of man as the struggle between good and evil. Every religion recognizes that tensions in the world are caused by the conflict between the forces of justice and injustice: "Each realizes that in the midst of the upward thrust of goodness there is the downward pull of evil." He insisted that one of the major tenets of Christianity is the idea that in the long struggle between good and evil, good will eventually triumph. Evil is doomed by the constant and inexorable forces of good. "This simply means that there is some good in the worst of us and some evil in the best of us."[35] Though evil carries the seeds of its own destruction, we must not relax our guard; "evil is recalcitrant and determined, and never voluntarily relinquishes its hold short of a persistent, almost fanatical resistance."[36] Nonetheless, it was his belief that there is a checkpoint in the universe and that evil cannot permanently sustain itself.[37]

The only way to overcome evil is through a unified cooperation between man and God. King asserted that neither man nor God would or could have removed evil alone, but both working together could cast evil out. No other way can rid the world of evil. Generally, King argues, man has sought to eradicate evil through his own ingenuity and power; through a belief in salvation, through progress and education. But clearly these attempts have failed. "In spite of . . . astounding new scientific developments, the old evils continue and the age of reason has been transformed into an age of terror. Selfishness and hatred have not vanished with an enlargement of our educational system and an extension of our legislative politics." That man can cast out evil by himself is a humanist idea overemphasizing the inherent goodness of human nature and suffering from excessive optimism. The humanists forget about man's capacity for sin, and history has shown the fallacy of this concept.

If one tendency in man's development has been to substitute human ingenuity for divine guidance, the other, according to King, expects God to do everything. It admonishes man to wait with patient submissiveness until God, in his own good time, would save the world. This notion, King felt, was rooted "in a pessimistic doctrine of human nature, which eliminated completely the capability of sinful man to do anything."[38] He felt that "the idea that man expects God to do everything leads inevitably to a callous misuse of prayer." For if man has but to ask and God will respond, then God becomes the servant of man—a "cosmic bellhop"—leaping to fulfill every whim and fancy of man, no matter how trivial. This view misconceives both man and God, making God a powerless despot and man a "helpless worm crawling through the morass of an evil world." In the final analysis, this point of view, King argues, is as untenable as it is pessimistic.

Since "man is neither totally depraved, nor God an almighty dictator, God will not do everything for man nor man do everything for himself." Neither alone will bring salvation to the world; but a unison of God and man could transform the venality of the human enterprise into an earthly heaven, and eliminate evil from all areas of human existence.[39]

King was, however, less concerned with the philo-

sophical explanation of evil than with its social manifestations. Only to the extent that evil, which invariably
results in the perversion of justice, is removed, can there
be evolution and progress in this world. Evil is the outcome of man's tragic misuse of his freedom, of his intellectual and moral blindness, and his failure to use his
mind to the fullest capacity.[40] To help preserve man
from his own calamities, King devised the moral strategy
of nonviolent resistance to regulate group life on a national and international scale. The first step, however,
had to lie with the individual and his moral regen-
eration; after the individual, then the group wherever
possible. At the heart of his philosophy of personalism
stood the individual, who, to become a good citizen and
genuinely nonviolent must live according to certain
ethical principles.

THE PSYCHOLOGICAL BASIS

All political theories rest on certain psychological assumptions regarding the nature of man from which his
behavior can then be interpreted and understood. King's
view of human nature was indissolubly linked with his
metaphysical and moral principles, accounting not only
for man's apparent behavior, but his spiritual or "true"
self as well.[41] He was concerned as much with what man
is capable of becoming, and how he might transform his
nature, as with his present state.

For a time, in his early development, King admitted
having wholly accepted the concept of human nature
advanced by liberalism, which held that men were innately good and naturally endowed with considerable
powers of reason.[42] Until, when he began to question
some of the theories associated with liberal theology, a

basic change in outlook occurred: "The more I observe the tragedies of history and man's shameful inclination to choose the low road, the more I can see the depths and strength of sin. Therefore, I realize that liberalism had been all too sentimental concerning human nature and that it leaned toward a false idealism." Liberalism failed also to see that human reason is frequently a captive of human emotion and, instead of guiding man's behavior, commonly ends up trying to justify it.

Both liberal theology and neo-orthodox views represented but a partial truth for King. While the former inclined toward an overly optimistic attitude regarding man's inherent goodness, the latter saw him only in terms of his actual fallen state. An adequate understanding of man would be one that would synthesize the truth of both views. King saw human nature to contain a mixture of good and evil; yet, when the individual enters into collective life, it is the evil that becomes more pronounced and tends to prevail. A basic dualism, then, a constant struggle between good and evil, is at work within man. In King's words:

> There is within human nature an amazing potential for goodness. There is within human nature something that can respond to goodness. I know somebody's liable to say that this is an unrealistic movement if it goes on believing that all people are good. Well, I didn't say that. I think . . . that there is a strange dichotomy of disturbing dualism within human nature. Many of the great philosophers and thinkers through the ages have seen this. . . . Plato, centuries ago said that the human personality is like a charioteer with two headstrong horses, each wanting to go in different directions, so that within our own individual lives we see this conflict and certainly when we come to the collective life of man, we see a strange badness.[43]

King, influenced by Niebuhr, felt that as a member of a group man sometimes behaves worse than when alone. With a sense of security and power which the numerical strength of his companions may give him, man loses his sense of responsibility, yields to the emotional appeal of the group and participates in activities and modes of behavior he would normally avoid. Thus the individual can be more amenable to reason and more alive to moral considerations than a group. Because the emphasis in group behavior tends to shift from inner purity to external conformity, a nonviolent group may not be as nonviolent, truthful, and loving as a nonviolent individual.[44] He had great faith, however, in the power of goodness to evoke a positive response in both groups and unregenerate individuals. Great moral leaders, such as Jesus and Gandhi could appeal to and bring forth the good in human beings, just as a Hitler could appeal to every potential for evil in them. Human nature, in other words, is susceptible to change; evil can be converted into good; the worst segregationist has the possibility of becoming an integrationist.[45] Even the most brutal of men cannot, according to King, entirely disown the spiritual element within themselves. For man is, above all, his soul, and possessed by an impulse to realize the inherent divinity of his true self. King also believed that human nature is in its essence one and that every man has the capacity for the highest possible development. This is why King emphasized the means rather than the end, effort rather than its fulfillment, and the necessity for ceaseless striving.

Imperfect but perfectible, man's nature can be molded and old habits reshaped by a conscious effort of will. If the technique of nonviolent resistance was to have any effect, it depended upon the underlying capacity of even the most hardened opponent being moved by the moral suffering of another, wholly truthful man. Through his own example and leadership, King showed that the development of conscious nonviolence is neither impossible nor impracticable, though it is a difficult ideal requiring constant effort and vigilance. He stressed the need of faith in nonviolence, adequate discipline, and self-purification if it was to succeed in influencing others. As a technique, nonviolence would entail suffering, but suffering King believed to be a part of human nature and essential for spiritual growth.[46] It was through suffering that the self-purification needed to develop one's human nature in a positive manner was achieved. And, since spiritual freedom means the capacity to love all, it also means to suffer all. To rise to the highest reaches of the ideal of suffering love is to rise to the highest potential of one's human nature. How exalted the ability to endure suffering had become in King's philosophy can be seen when he declared in a speech given after the Montgomery boycott:

> We will match your capacity [that of whites] to inflict suffering with our capacity to endure suffering. We will meet your physical force with soul force. . . . Do to us what you will and we will still love you. Bomb our homes and threaten our children; send your hooded perpetrators of violence into our communities and drag us out on some wayside road, beating us and leaving us half dead, and we will still love you. But we will soon wear you down by our capacity to suffer.[47]

He further stated:

> The way of nonviolence means a willingness to suffer and sacrifice. It may mean going to jail. If such is the case the resistor must be willing to fill the jail houses of the South. It may even mean physical death. But if

physical death is the price that a man must pay to free his children and his white brethren from a permanent death of the spirit, then nothing more could be more redemptive.[48]

Unearned suffering is, therefore, redemptive, and to suffer in a creative way serves to transform the social situation. This emphasis upon the redemptive role of suffering stems from King's belief in a Christianity which teaches voluntary submission to sacrifice, privation, and the renunciation of external happiness. Christ's death upon the cross was perceived by King as a means by which the gates to paradise were opened.[49] The attainment of a better future on earth is therefore dependent upon continuous suffering. Often, even the mere anticipation of suffering prepares the way to the fulfillment of otherwise forbidden values, such as the good life for Negroes.

Summarizing then, King felt that through suffering and sacrifice one can become uncommonly noble, gentle, and heroic. It enables one to feel that "we are, after all, the better men," "better" in the moral and spiritual sense. And finally, it is a means whereby one may realize the highest possible potential of his human nature.

THE RELATION OF MEANS TO ENDS

In King's philosophy the means are as important as the ends: in practice, they are inseparable. So too, lofty purposes must be attained by equally moral means. King strongly repudiated the notion that the ends can justify the means; the one is as good or as perverted as the other. Unjust means, ostensibly in the service of just ends, are frequently used to permit violence, fraud, untruth, opportunism, etc. Rather than helping us toward progress, foul means teach us to regard human beings as mere instruments, deaden our finer feelings, and result in oppression and cruelty. This he saw in communism, which holds that the ends justifies the means. Although communist theory postulates the transformation to a classless society, it permits any method—no matter how cruel or unjust—to achieve this praiseworthy end. In fact, the individual under communism finds himself utterly subjugated to the state, because the state—not man—is what is most valued. King, however, asserts that the state is made for man and not vice-versa. Wherever the state is allowed to become an end in itself, any act, no matter how vile, is nonetheless given sanction.[50]

According to King, man, because he is a child of God, is an end in himself.[51] To use man in the manner the communists would use him is to deprive him of his freedom and relegate him to the status of a thing. Treated as a mere means, man loses sight of his relationship with God, his spiritual qualities, and becomes a non-person.[52] Inherent in the philosophy of nonviolent direct action is the belief that the ends are preexistent in the means: a community of love and brotherhood could only come into being through the fully moral behavior of many individuals.

Violence, on the other hand, King viewed as both immoral and impractical since it could achieve but temporary successes at best.[53] Violence can never secure a state of permanent peace since it continues to generate new and more complicated problems than the ones it aims to solve. It generates a legacy of negative feeling that perpetuates conflict rather than reconciliation. As a method of achieving racial justice, violence clings to the old law of an eye for an eye, until all parties are blind and eventually destroyed. Because it humiliates and annihilates the opponent, rather than attempting to convert or understand him, violence is immoral. Thriving on hate, it destroys true community and confines the members of society to a monologue of bitterness from those who survive its reaches and brutality to those who use it to destroy.[54]

There are, according to King, three ways in which to deal with the problem of oppression. People can fight it using violent means issuing in a perpetual state of fear and destruction; they can acquiesce, or they can choose the means of nonviolent direct action. Acquiescence to the conditions of oppression is also, King felt, immoral and, in the long run, impractical. By resigning oneself, by adjusting to the forces of oppression, one is implicitly cooperating with the evil within the environment. The refusal to take action means a passive acceptance of segregation and injustice, which is tantamount to saying that the oppressor is morally right. Inaction then, while often the easier way, is not the moral way but the way of the coward.[55] Its impracticality lies in its allowing an evil system to continue, possibly "hoping for the best," while all that can come of such conditions is more of the same.

Clearly then, in King's view, only the way of nonviolent direct action can help oppressed people in their quest for freedom, for only it combines and reconciles the tendencies toward violence and acquiescence "while avoiding the extremes and immoralities of both." The nonviolent resister accepts—like the person who acquiesces—that physical force should not be used against an opponent and combines with it the violent person's reaction that evil must not go unresisted. By the use of nonviolent techniques no group or individual need either submit to oppression or retaliate violently. Logically, therefore, the only moral and practical means to end oppression, and the only systematic way of reacting that can lead to lasting peace and progress, is nonviolent resistance and direct action. This basically ethical outlook forms the backbone of King's political philosophy, just as his ethical principles formed the basis for his metaphysics. To him, the moral discipline of the individual was the most important means of social reconstruction and it is the cornerstone of his entire philosophy.

THE CONCEPT OF SOCIAL PROGRESS

The phenomena of political and social change are, in King's philosophy, tied to his idea of the dialectic: "The dialectical process . . . helped me to see that growth comes through struggle."[56] Progress comes through a struggle that begins with a confrontation between what is and what ought to be, through the experience of what he termed "creative tension," a nonviolent tension that he considered necessary for growth.[57] An absence of tension, in his view, means stagnation and complacency. For the simple reason that human progress is not automatic or inevitable, it will not come about without a struggle, with pressure exerted on the status quo.

A glance at human history, King believed, reveals that the pursuit of justice and equality requires not only continual exertion, concern, and dedicated individuals, but sacrifice, suffering, and struggle. Time, together with perseverance, becomes a powerful force for motion and social progress.[58] As he saw it, no privileged group would give up its position without resisting strongly. Creative suffering, on the part of those attacking the privileged, helps also to transform the social situation. Every attempt to change the status quo should be moral;

hence, nonviolence should be the method employed. Moreover, the struggle implicit in any effort toward social progress, if it is to succeed, must be unified with God. Only with the tireless efforts of men in unison with God is triumph assured.

NONVIOLENT CIVIL DISOBEDIENCE

Within this framework of assumptions and beliefs, nonviolent civil disobedience fitted as no other form of political action could have. It furnished the "arm" for all of King's political tactics; the means for keeping the government "stirred to life," and it was morally right and obligatory. More than a philosophical posture, nonviolence was for him a way of life, one that men adopt out of recognition of the sheer morality of its claim. As a rule, King held, if a person is willing to use nonviolence as a technique, he is likely to adopt it later as a way of life.[59]

King firmly believed that as a method of civil disobedience, nonviolent resistance and direct action is the most potent weapon available to oppressed people in their struggle for freedom and human dignity. It is a way of disarming the opponent, exposing his moral weaknesses, undermining his morale, and, at the same time, affecting his conscience.[60] It paralyzes and confuses the power structure against which it is directed, while it endows its initiators with a new sense of self-respect, duty, strength, devotion, courage, and dignity.[61] To employ the method of nonviolence, one must be very strong spiritually; spiritual strength is the opposite of the shirking passivity associated with cowardice. Strictly speaking, nonviolence does not defeat the opponent, but tries to win his friendship and understanding.

Also characteristic of nonviolence, according to King, is that it attacks evil itself, rather than the evildoer. A nonviolent person resisting the evils of racial injustice can see that the basic tension is not between the races, but "between justice and injustice, between the force of light and the force of darkness." Through the willing acceptance of suffering without retaliation the nonviolent resister attempts to overcome by the power of his persistent love the intransigence of the oppressor. Violence and punishment must be tolerated by the peaceful resister, for, though he may hate the deed, he must love the perpetrator of that deed.

As King interpreted it, nonviolent resistance derives from the conviction that justice abounds in the universe, and that this justice works on the side of the nonviolent resister. He has, therefore, a deep faith in the future outcome of his struggle for justice since he carries with him the awareness that he has "cosmic companionship."[62] In sum, King's nonviolence sought simultaneously to: resist; defeat an unjust system; attack evil but not the evildoer; make suffering a virtue; love rather than hate; and create faith in God and the future. And, for him, the techniques of nonviolence offered every possible moral and ethical way, both internally and externally, to achieve these ends.

It was King's great hope that blacks would, as they plunged deeper into the quest for freedom, come ever closer to the philosophy of nonviolence. For blacks especially, in his view, have a mission as well as an obligation to work "passionately and unrelentingly for first-class citizenship," without, of course, resorting to violence to achieve this end. Just as passivity on the part of blacks would earn for them increased disrespect, contempt, and be interpreted as proof of their inferiority, so would violence leave future generations a heritage of racial bitterness and meaningless chaos. Whereas, with nonviolent techniques passionately and unrelentingly applied, it would be possible for blacks to remain in the South and work for full status as citizens. They would also thereby absolve themselves from the perpetuation of hate, malice, and involvement with the forces of evil. With a nonviolent foundation, King conceived that the black struggle in the South could also serve as a model for oppressed people everywhere. Blacks could then enlist to their side men of good will from all parts of the world, because nonviolence addresses itself to the conscience of men, not to racial groups or individuals.[63]

By overcoming the personal feelings of resentment which might otherwise be expressed in retaliation and hatred, the nonviolent resister develops an internal strength and discipline that is not of the body but of the soul. Those qualities, in other words, assumed to convert the oppressor to a greater sense of respect and justice for his "fellow in God." The soul-force of nonviolent resistance, King claimed, affects the adversary unconsciously and in a way far greater than any conscious effect. Thus, in reality then, nonviolence is potentially the most active force in the world. It has the additional advantage of being self-activating and independent of any outside physical force.

For King, there could be no question of defeat. For what is obtained by love is retained for all time; whereas what is obtained through hatred becomes a burden, for it breeds more hatred. In a nonviolent struggle there are no casualties. The victory is complete because the method used is not coercive. To be nonviolent is to be God-like. Thus, to use nonviolence in any struggle against injustice is to do the will of God and to be His representative as well. In King's words:

> Nonviolence is a powerful and just weapon. It is a weapon unique in history, which cuts without wounding and ennobles the man who wields it. It is a sword that heals. Both a practical and a moral answer to the Negro's cry for justice, nonviolent direct action proved that it could win victories without losing wars.[64]

However, merely to accept the concept of nonviolence is, according to King, not enough. The "love ethic" brings nonviolence into another dimension and makes of it a way of life. King readily saw that many people would accept nonviolence in certain situations as the most practical method, but he felt that it was necessary for them also to follow the love ethic "which becomes a force of personality integration."[65] The love of which he spoke was not a sentimental or affectionate emotion, but understanding and redemptive good will.

To clarify the nature of the love he had in mind, King compared the three Greek words for love: eros, philia, and agape. Eros refers to romantic or aesthetic love; philia is a reciprocal love, the kind that may exist between close friends; agape is a dispassionate, redemptive love that embraces all men. Agape is an overflowing love "which seeks nothing in return, it is the love of God operating in the human heart." On this level of love, man can love his enemies while yet hating their actions.[66] "It is a love in which the individual seeks not his own good, but the good of his neighbor."[67] Nondiscriminating, seeking the best in every man, agape springs from the need of every person to belong to the best of the human family.[68] The highest principle, for King, was love, for only through a certain kind of love, agape, would there be the constant willingness to sacrifice in the interest of mutuality; the willingness to forgive, over and over again, as many times as necessary; and the possibility of restoring the broken fragments of community. Because King felt that segregation had greatly distorted the white man's personality and scarred his soul, he needed the love of black people to repair these damages which only love could cure.

In the final analysis then, agape, for King means "a recognition of the fact that all life is interrelated." On another level, this interrelationship of all humanity implies union within a single process of harmony and brotherhood that persists regardless of the acts of individual men who may work against it. "To the degree that I harm my brother no matter what he is doing to me, to that extent I am harming myself." To love, King felt, is to resist injustice, to meet the needs of your brother, to restore community, and to be God-like.

But how does this nonviolent love ethic become a political motivation directed toward changing the status quo? The hierarchy of a citizen's loyalties is explicitly stated by King:

> Your highest loyalty is to God, and not to the mores or folkways, the state or the nation or any man-made institution. If any earthly institution or custom conflicts with God's will, it is your Christian duty to oppose it. You must never allow the transitory, evanescent demands of man-made institutions to take precedence over the eternal demands of the almighty God.[69]

A righteous man, therefore, to be true to his conscience and true to God, has no alternative but to refuse to cooperate with a system judged to be evil. And, since his oppressor may not recognize the nature and extent of his own injustice if it is accepted without protest, the obligation to act forcefully on the side of good is mandatory.

Segregation, for example, was viewed by King as not only politically, economically, and socially unsound, but as morally wrong because it has the deeper effect of distorting the soul and damaging the personality. Refusal to cooperate with a segregated system can take various forms of nonviolent civil disobedience, which, if accomplished in the spirit of the love ethic, work to right existing wrongs while, at the same time, are in harmony with the direction of human progress and the community of men. On a practical level, nonviolent civil action can breathe life into civil rights legislation granted Negroes on paper but absent in reality; thus proving, according to King, an ideal and unique way for the Negro to attain social justice and equality.

Again, within the framework of democracy, where the legal means to redress grievances has been perverted, nonviolent civil disobedience proves itself to be the only practical and moral way to gain permanent change. In King's mind there was an equal moral responsibility to obey just laws as there was to disobey unjust ones. The difference between the two lay in the latter's being out of harmony with eternal, natural law, or the law of God. "I would agree with Saint Augustine that 'an unjust law is no law' at all." Attempting to give a concrete example of just and unjust laws, King explained:

> An unjust law is a code that a numerical or powerful majority group compels a minority group to obey but does not make it binding on itself. This is *difference* made legal. By the same token, a just law is a code that a majority compels a minority to follow and that it is willing to follow itself. This is sameness made legal.[70]

Giving still more explicit expression to this definition,

King went even further when he stated that "A law is unjust if it is inflicted on a minority . . . that has been denied the right to vote and had no part in enacting or devising the law." In other words, when a minority is excluded from the total democratic process, as the Negroes in Alabama and Mississippi were, then the laws of these states cannot be considered just. "Any law enacted under such circumstances cannot be considered democratically structured."[71] Further, a law may be just on the surface and unjust in its application.[72] An example of this would be denying Negroes the right to use a parade permit as a way of maintaining segregation. This would be a situation calling for acts of nonviolent protest.

King made an added distinction between civil disobedience and uncivil disobedience. The former was represented by those who sat-in, the latter by the rabid segregationist who defies, evades, or circumvents those laws he considers inimical to his personal prejudices. Unwilling to accept the penalty for his defiance of the law, his violation ends in anarchy and a show of utter disrespect for the law. The nonviolent student protester, on the other hand, willingly accepts the penalty for a law he disobeys because his conscience tells him that it is unjust. By his actions, his willingness to remain in jail until the law is changed, the student shows his respect for the law. King stressed the importance of disobeying unjust laws with a willingness to accept whatever penalty the law then imposes, so that the public would then come to reexamine the law in question and decide whether it was uplifting or degrading.[73]

In sum, while disobedience is in itself destructive and antisocial, obedience to an immoral law is even worse and should always be opposed. A law, to be worthy of obedience, must be moral and democractically formulated. In extreme cases in a democracy, if a citizen cannot obtain the repeal of an immoral law through constitutional means, he should disobey the law as an act of conscience and willingly accept the penalty for having done so. Nonviolent civil disobedience, in King's view, was an effort to reconcile the demands of freedom and law, justice and democratic process, this world and that to come.

THE BELOVED COMMUNITY

Figuring throughout King's writings is the idea of a beloved community,[74] reminiscent of Saint Augustine's City of God, Gandhi's nonviolent state, Saint Aquinas' City of Righteousness, and, to some extent, Rousseau's social contract: each an example of how the moral imagination has sought to delineate the perfect social community. King's beloved community differs from those of his predecessors in its adoption of nonviolence as an imperative, and not a mere policy. For nonviolence acts to reestablish the wholeness of community, reconcile the oppressor with the oppressed, and create a brotherhood of blacks and whites.

However, nowhere in his writing did King attempt to define or give structure to his vision of a beloved community. The implication was that it would emerge spontaneously as the byproduct of the practice of nonviolence at that period in history when people have acquired true self-control, total cooperation, and complete trust in God. Discussing the idea of a beloved community, King constantly stressed that one had first to be willing to suffer for his brother's sake, that one must express love (agape) to its fullest extent, and live with devotion, concern for justice, rightness, and harmony with God. These are the guiding ideals that will hasten the coming of the beloved community and ensure its survival. Because violence, hate, fear, and deceit are what shatter a community, man must have evolved beyond the rule of his lower self to the principle of love. The method of nonviolence and the highest ethical and moral principles would constitute the communal order.[75] In the beloved community evil will have disappeared along with the tensions of hate, insecurity, and inferiority: through total commitment to brotherhood, injustices will vanish. Evidence of the great faith King placed in the harmony generated by reliance on God, love, and nonviolence in man's dealings with his fellowman, was his conviction that through these forces a utopian society would come into being, admittedly a "dream," but the only one worthy of striving toward.

SOME PRACTICAL CONSIDERATIONS

King admitted that the struggle of mankind's minorities for justice and full equality, particularly in America, can be supplemented by means other than nonviolent resistance and direct action. This could take the form of favorable legislation, strong federal leadership, political alliances, and self-help: direct action, in his view, was not a substitute for work in the courts and chambers of government. Since the nation's greatest merit rests on its being a government of laws and not of men, many of the difficulties inherent in a democratically functioning government would have to be accepted. The task of nonviolent action was to spur indifferent, complacent institutions into taking appropriate measures for change.

New legislation, King felt, could help to overcome discrimination by imposing criteria with which to regulate the policies of organizations, by, for example, issuing sanctions against employers refusing to hire blacks on the basis of color alone.[76] Laws and legal decisions, by creating new standards, could affect the patterns of conduct which would eventually alter people's social habits. And, over a period of time, King hoped, altered habits might lead to more fundamental changes in beliefs and attitudes.[77] However, the enactment of favorable civil rights legislation was by itself not enough: it would have to be backed up with the readiness to use federal power to enforce such laws whenever and wherever necessary. There was also the danger of the authority of the federal government diminishing in the eyes of many if it persistently ignored the infringements of its mandates at the state, county, and municipal levels. Only by the combined efforts of comprehensive laws backed by the positive leadership of government could constitutional mandates be made meaningful and those committed to resisting equal rights be moved to comply.

What is more, federal action, in King's opinion, needed to be both swift and complete: "It is the obligation of the government to move resolutely to the side of the freedom movement. There is a right and a wrong side in this conflict and the government does not belong in the middle." He also argued that America had to atone for the way she had permitted her minorities to be treated, suggesting a "bill of rights for the disadvantaged," similar to the veterans' bill of rights, except that it would be more broadly based and larger in scope.[78] Such a bill, King thought, would if enacted immediately transform the conditions of Negro life.

In addition to this bill, King felt that the chief executive should use the power of his office to institute measures promoting equality and justice for minorities

whenever Congress reached an impasse, or for some reason failed to act.[79] During the centennial celebration of
the Emancipation Proclamation, King took the opportunity to present to the President an appeal entitled
"An Appeal to the President of the United States for
National Rededication to the Principles of the Emancipation Proclamation," which called upon President
Kennedy to use his executive powers to the utmost to
remove every form of segregation and discrimination
from the United States. King also called upon the chief
executive to lead the country to becoming aware of the
black man's plight and his need for justice and to ask
the country to aid him in his quest.[80] It was the responsibility of the government to undertake the initiation of
legal proceedings on behalf of the poor and unem-
ployed, since the accumulation of resources needed to
institute legal action imposed yet another hardship on
those already overburdened.

To be added to the efforts of the government and the
chief executive was the help that could come from alliances of blacks and other like-minded disadvantaged
groups. Labor was one group sharing similar problems
and a similar oppression to blacks with which King
thought that an alliance would serve to strengthen the
positions of both. Or, should a schism occur between
Negroes and organized labor, "Nothing," in his view,
"would hold back the forces of progress in American
life more effectively."

King also advocated economic self-help, the establishment of black-owned businesses, cooperative owner-
ship, and credit unions, as another means whereby blacks
could work toward equality. Besides initiating business
enterprises, King asserted that blacks needed to acquire
the habits of thrift and the techniques of wise invest-

ment, advice echoing the words of Booker T. Washington. Unlike Washington, however, King did not believe that constitutional rights for blacks would flow automatically from their success in the business world, but definitely needed the additional means of black political power actively engaged in the work of liberation.

The personal standards of many black people disturbed King and he recommended that a vigorous attempt be made to improve upon their moral, spiritual, and social character. He specifically criticized the high black crime rate, the failure of the black middle class to support adequately black organizations, excessive drinking, and the uncouth public behavior frequently displayed by blacks.

What is remarkable about these suggestions and criticisms is not their originality, since most of them had been derived from earlier thinkers, but their total congruence within the framework of King's moral philosophy: everywhere a scrupulous attempt is made to avoid any discrepancy between theory and practice, between the ideal and what can be made real. The overall vision is always one of action within a potentially harmonious whole, an orchestration of roles directed toward moral ends. Asserting that blacks should form alliances with the most powerful and like-minded groups in the country, he was emphasizing the interrelatedness of all groups and their need to bring about social progress through mutual endeavor. Since whatever affects the part also affects the whole, if blacks are disadvantaged, deprived, and suffering, then the rest of society is in some way, to some degree, likewise afflicted. If society is to move upward, if it is to undergo the rejuvenation it so drastically needs, then all its members, using all the resources available, must work together as harmoniously as possible.

The means chosen to attack the system should not destroy the system, but help shape it, inch by inch if need be, into a better world.

NOTES

1. Myrdal, *An American Dilemma,* pp. 28, 781, 786.
2. Loewenstein, "Political Systems, Ideologies, and Institutions."
3. King, *Stride Toward Freedom,* p. 90. See also "Pilgrimage to Nonviolence," p. 439.
4. Clayton, *The Peaceful Warrior,* p. 39.
5. King, *Stride Toward Freedom,* p. 91.
6. Ibid.
7. Ibid., pp. 96–97.
8. King, *Strength to Love,* p. 141.
9. Ibid.
10. Ibid., p. 169.
11. Ibid., p. 99.
12. Ibid., p. 101.
13. Ibid.
14. Ibid., p. 101.
15. Reddick, *Crusader Without Violence,* p. 14.
16. King, *Stride Toward Freedom,* p. 93.
17. King, "A Comparison of the Conception of God in the Thinking of Paul Tillich and Henry Nelson Wieman," p. 141.
18. King, *Stride Toward Freedom,* p. 36.
19. King, *Strength to Love,* pp. 114–118.
20. Ibid., p. 4, italics mine.
21. King, "The Un-Christian Christian."
22. King, *Strength to Love,* pp. 118–119
23. Ibid., p. 11.
24. Ibid.
25. King, "The Most Durable Power."
26. King, *Strength to Love,* p. 78.
27. Reddick, *Crusader Without Violence,* p. 23.
28. King, "Love, Law and Civil Disobedience," p. 7.
29. King, "A Comparison of the Conception of God in Tillich and Wieman."

30. King, *Strength to Love*, p. 142.

31. Ibid., p. 45.

32. Ibid., p. 47.

33. Ibid., p. 110.

34. Ibid., p. 99.

35. Ibid.

36. Ibid.

37. Ibid.

38. Ibid.

39. King, *The Measure of a Man*, pp. 32–33.

40. King, *Strength to Love*, pp. 147–152.

41. King, *The Measure of a Man*, pp. 1–16.

42. King, *Strength to Love*, pp. 165, 106–113. See also *Measure of a Man*, chap. 1.

43. King, "Love, Law and Civil Disobedience," p. 6.

44. King, *Strength to Love*, pp. 10–19.

45. King, "Love, Law and Civil Disobedience," p. 6.

46. King, *Strength to Love*, pp. 30–31.

47. King, *Stride Toward Freedom*, p. 217.

48. King, "A Comparison of the Conception of God in Tillich and Wieman," p. 216.

49. King, *Strength to Love*, pp. 30–33.

50. Ibid., p. 116.

51. King, *Stride Toward Freedom*, p. 93.

52. Ibid.

53. Ibid., pp. 212–213.

54. Ibid., p. 213.

55. Ibid., p. 212.

56. Ibid., p. 101.

57. King, *Why We Can't Wait*, p. 81.

58. King, *Stride Toward Freedom*, p. 197.

59. Ibid., p. 89.

60. Ibid., p. 219.

61. Ibid., p. 217.

62. Ibid., pp. 102–104, 107–117.

63. King, "The Case Against Tokenism," p. 3; see also Lewis, *Portrait of the Decade*, p. 83.

64. King, *Why We Can't Wait*, p. 14.

65. King, "An Interview," in Clark, ed., *The Negro Protest*, pp. 39–40.

66. King, "Love, Law and Civil Disobedience," p. 5.

67. King, *Stride Toward Freedom,* p. 104.

68. Ibid.

69. King, *Strength to Love,* p. 108.

70. King, *Why We Can't Wait,* pp. 68–69.

71. King, "Love, Law and Disobedience," p. 8.

72. King, *Why We Can't Wait,* p. 86.

73. King, "The Time for Freedom Has Come," p. 2.

74. References to the idea of a beloved community occur throughout King's writings, but it is most extensively discussed in *Stride Toward Freedom,* esp. pp. 102–106, 189–224.

75. King, *Stride Toward Freedom,* p. 106.

76. King, "Behind the Selma March."

77. King, "The Case Against Tokenism," p. 3.

78. King, *Why We Can't Wait,* pp. 148–151.

79. King, "Equality Now"; see also *A Martin Luther King Treasury,* pp. 289–335.

80. King, *A Martin Luther King Treasury,* pp. 289–335. The section on the appeal sets forth the various ways past executive orders have succeeded and outlines a way of approaching the president legally to issue such an order.

4 | *The Way of Nonviolence: A Critical View*

BEFORE beginning a critical analysis of King's political philosophy, some remarks are in order. There is no denying the success his theory of nonviolent direct action has had in gaining for the Negro some measure of civil rights, or its psychological impact upon the black man himself, the sense of dignity, self-respect, and personal worth it has given him. The leadership and oratorical skill King displayed in articulating and putting into practice his ideas has also to be hailed. How much his personality, political philosophy, and actions did to change race relations in this country can hardly be overestimated. Nonetheless, the implications of his nonviolent ethic, both as a philosophic and strategic posture, raise as many questions as that ethic sought to answer.

To exercise a critical view is not, of course, to discredit either the man or his theory, but rather to seek and perhaps find new points of departure applicable to the present stage of the black minorities' continuing social struggle. If critical analysis points to the weaknesses inherent in a particular philosophical stance, it likewise points to its strength. Regardless of the shortcomings in their theories, mankind has learned much from Plato, Aristotle, Hobbes, and Marx. Their ideas, or at least the best parts of their ideas, continue to yield fresh insights into the possibilities existing in our changing world.

Similarly, it is hoped that an evaluation of King's political philosophy will provide new insight into the individual's relationship to government and the political imagination acting to transform those relationships.

We might begin by examining the concept of agape, the selfless, redemptive love which King considered essential for the nonviolent resister. By what standards or criteria is the practice of this or for that matter any other form of love to be judged? Unfortunately, King gives us no indication; we are left simply with a definition drawn, at that, from classical Greek texts, and a moral imperative directed toward all who would practice nonviolence.

Has experience borne out the contention that nonviolence to be effective must be combined with the highest kind of love? Judging from the work of CORE and other groups that have used nonviolent direct action with excellent results, the answer is an unequivocal no. Considering the difficulty encountered by most people in attempting to fuse the highest form of love of which they are capable with any form of political action, even nonviolent action, how can we account for King's insistence upon this fusion as the *only* effective strategy in the long run? The explanation seems to lie in the fear of uncontrolled violence and hate which more militant tactics might unleash. It has even been suggested that the injunction to "love thy neighbor" was introduced to serve in the control of social strife and physical violence.[1] Rather than constituting a wholly positive or "giving" force, it can also be seen as a negative force for the prevention and control of destructive conflict.

Further, since all human actions are conditional and relative, none is exclusively agape. In the same way, the choice of nonviolent political techniques is itself part of a larger, more complex social process in which no single element can be artificially isolated as "pure." Nor is access to the special influence of agape granted by reason or nature, for it is not an abstraction to be applied at will, a self-generating power, or one that can be made to serve a purpose other than its own. To be truly itself it must come from God as the gift of His grace; our human role is but that of recipient and transmitter.

Some critics have found in this disinterested and lofty role love is given in King's political philosophy a refusal to participate in the claims and counterclaims of historical instances.[2] Doubts arise as to whether an objectless love is able to maintain itself in a historical setting without falling victim to others' excessive forms of self-assertion. According to Reinhold Niebuhr, a life devoted to this ideal of love must end in tragedy. The closest we can actually come to realizing justice is through the balance of competing wills and interests, which are liable to destroy whatever does not compete or assert itself.[3] If we accept the truth of the foregoing view it becomes evident that the functions assigned to agape in King's political philosophy stand little chance of surviving, much less proving fruitful, in the real world.

Equally, it is questionable whether the ordinary person is capable of achieving the agape level of love. Can modern men, characteristically self-centered and aggressive, overcome these qualities and attain the transcendent love symbolized by Christ on the cross?

The failure of this higher spiritual love becomes increasingly apparent as one moves from the individual to the group. King's own recognition of the tendency for groups to behave less morally than individuals runs directly counter to his expectation in another context of collective agape. How realistic is it to expect of people united for basically political purposes a standard of love normally out of reach of all but the most singular of them?

King stressed that one is able to love a person while hating the deeds of that person. But how much of a person can actually be separated from his actions? And who, if not that person, is to be held responsible for those actions? For good as well as for evil acts, are there not important differences of degree and kind? How are these distinctions to be made? How is the evil perpetrated by one person to be distinguished from that bred by social institutions and their conditioning effects? On these recurrent questions King's philosophy is silent.

When we examine King's own use of love how truly selfless and disinterested do we find it to be? Did he not seek something, however worthy, in return; namely, equality, freedom, and personal dignity? Was not the entire nonviolent ethic a way of creating new terms for a give and take between social groups, and as such a purposive and intensely "interested" exchange?

To impose a pure love ethic in a realm where, at best, only relative justice can be attained is a utopian attempt.[4] The perfection of agape symbolized by Christ on the Cross transcends all particular norms of justice and mutuality in history; it seeks conformity with divine love, rather than confluence with other human interests. To elevate harmony to a final norm, which appears to be King's position, instead of a desirable end, is also to diminish the ethical purity of this love. For man's egoism and self-interest tend to render all historical harmonies of interest partial and incomplete. Therefore, to attempt to attain harmony as a final rather than a desirable end, is to seek the impossible.

Both King's concept of love and his embodiment of it had an overwhelming attraction to that "something" within human nature which responds to goodness. Acknowledging this, King stated that a Jesus of Nazareth or a Mahatma Gandhi can appeal to that element of goodness, just as a Hitler can appeal to that element of evil within men. But is this not a crucial oversimplification of the historical reality? Are we to believe that only great leaders can call forth a high order of goodness or its opposite? Is the vast majority of mankind to be consigned to the status of a sleeping mammal, roused to significant action only at the prodding of a few? To adopt a view that man's history, moral or otherwise, is dependent upon the leadership of a few, is to despair for mankind.

Lacking evidence for the ability of King's ethic of love to move the power structure to the extent he believed it could, we nonetheless do have examples of nonviolent protest succeeding in its aims quite independent of the presence or absence of the element of love. Through such concrete measures as court injunctions, economic boycotts, pickets, a strong and vocal press, sit-ins, and allied tactics, gains for equal rights have been made. White southern merchants have shown themselves to be not in the least indifferent to the commercial value of the black man. While they are aware that the black man's buying power is on a per capita basis less than the white man's, still, the aggregate is too large to be ignored.

In the face of hard economic facts, does one need the addition of a love ethic to the message spelled out by boycotts and demonstrations? For King the answer is an unqualified yes, but nowhere in his speeches or writings does he cite reasons why this might be so. Nor does he allow for alternative attitudes to that of a highly idealized, for most mortals impossible goal of love.

At the opposite pole, King insisted that violence was intrinsically wrong and its use could in no case be morally justified. Others, however, have persuasively argued that this is itself a dubious assumption and that "nothing is intrinsically immoral except ill-will and nothing intrinsically good except good-will."[5] It is quite possible to conceive of the controlled use of violent means working for highly legitimate ends, but here as in all discussions of violence, it is important to define clearly what we mean by the term. Should changes considered to be good be accomplished by means less than perfect, as most human processes are, the capacity for those changes to continue effectuating "good" is not thereby limited. A complexity of circumstances and human subjectivities enter at every stage of change, coloring and shaping what eventuates with a variety of motives which any one of us would be hard-pressed to distinguish for the measure of "good" or "evil."

According to Webster, violence is defined as "an intent to compel one to do something by forceful means." The Oxford Universal Dictionary defines it as "the exercise of physical force so as to inflict injury on or damage to person or property; a spiritual violation of the person or his relations." But whether physical or spiritual, violence connotes destructiveness, which, when it affects persons, is evil.[6] There is also a kind of psychological violence, committed by acts physical and nonphysical, which do injury to the integrity and dignity of individuals. Clearly, violence can assume many forms; physical, economic, spiritual, psychological, and countless subtle variations of these. Which raises the question whether it is possible to expunge every taint of violence from one's actions, however well-intentioned they be. Does not nonviolence as well as violence coerce by the pressures it brings to bear upon persons not yet ready for a radical change of outlook?

The benefits to be derived from the practice of non-violence are, in King's view, dual: the improvement of the social order and the perfecting of its practitioner's soul. The path to human perfectibility is seen along the way of unearned suffering, of absorbing, as it were, the violence of negative emotions from others. But is it reasonable to expect of men whose character in no way resembles that of Jesus or Gandhi that they always respond acceptingly, unresistingly, to the thrusts and attacks of their fellow men? Or when people have undergone systematic dehumanization—as in the Nazi concentration camps—are stoicism and love what we should expect from them? And when the Ku Klux Klan and the rabid segregationists ignore the black man's creative suffering, and even respond with renewed energies of hate, is universal love an appropriate or an elevating response? Do we lack in examples of the modern exercise of brute force where the practitioners, if they even bother to note the conduct of their target victims, consider human reactions totally irrelevant to the execution of their aims?

It has long been observed that the more dehumanized people become, the closer they are to viewing others as mere symbols. The "other" comes to represent an abstraction deemed undesirable and less than human; in this purview the particular reactions of the object–victims can have no modifying effect since, to begin with, they do not wholly exist. Dehumanization can play more complex tricks with the psyche than a Christian ethic of love and redemptive suffering can perhaps adequately deal with. Noting that many whites experience severe psychological difficulty in dealing with this "strange love" shown them by black people, Lillian Smith relates that compassion from someone whom you consider beneath you or whom you have harmed, is enraging. One can respond to humor, behave justly, and relate to compassion only in situations where justice, compassion, and humor are valued.[7] If this is so, then there are only certain circumstances under which people can respond at all, much less compassionately, to their fellow man's suffering. Yet, King remained firmly convinced that creative suffering would bring about social change.

Equally vulnerable to the cold light of historical experience is King's conviction that nonviolence, beyond being a political strategy and moral weapon, is a way of life whereby all conflicts between men can be resolved. But even a casual analysis of the conditions under which it has succeeded reveals their highly special character. Working within a religious framework, men like King and Gandhi were able to use this method first of all within societies where their voices already commanded wide respect and where their pronouncements were assured widespread publicity. The measures they advocated found ready support from the ruling classes and they could appeal to the humanitarian ideals of the dominant group. These special features and others leave little doubt as to whether nonviolence would be effective or even relevant in all situations. How, for example, in a tradition devoid of respect for the individual, can nonviolence be effective? Or under a totalitarian or repressive regime? Against the committed racists of Southern Rhodesia and South Africa? Barring a universal moral revolution, little change in the chances for nonviolent strategies succeeding in these and other situations can be reasonably expected.

Is it not also fair to say that the ever-present threat of violence has been crucial to the acceptance of nonviolent strategies where they have succeeded? Were not the leaders of nonviolent movements constantly reminding their opponents that if their demands were not met, they might not be able to restrain their followers, or those who would follow them. Certainly this is true of King. As early as 1961 when he felt that something needed to be done about the emerging frustrations of blacks in the large industrial areas of the North,[8] King went on to warn his opponents that black Muslims were ready and willing to exploit those frustrations.[9] The question is whether any nonviolent campaign can succeed without the implicit threat of violence from more radical sources. And whether it is possible for any movement to wholly dissociate itself from the coercive extreme of violence.

Many think not. The need for the presence of a more violent threat to activate social change has been corroborated by H. L. Nieburg who notes the need for an implied ultimatum of violence to make nonviolence an acceptable alternative to those in power.[10] The very distinction so strenuously upheld between violence and nonviolence is annihilated by Niebuhr in his refusal to overlook the element of coercion common to both.[11] If consequences are not confused with intentions, we can see the similarities as well as the differences between nonviolent and violent means: both, though starting with different intentions and differing in the character of their execution, may result in the destruction of property and life.

In defending nonviolence against an imputed associ-

ation with violence, King drew the parallel of the condemning of a robbed man on the grounds that his pos-
session of money precipitated the crime of robbery, and
the condemnation of Jesus on the basis of his devotion
to God's will which then precipitated the violent act of
crucifixion.[12] As Howard Zinn has pointed out, nonviolence theorists will insist on placing responsibility for
violence at the feet of those who commit such acts rather
than admit its having any relationship with their particular movement. Evidence to this effect was that following the start of the Freedom Rides there was much
more overt violence than there had been before. The
one justification cited by the nonviolent practitioners
was that compared with the justice won, the amount of
violence was insignificant.[13]

Another gloss on the superior virtue of nonviolence
stems from King's tendency to value it as an absolute
good, as the highest civil and political morality. But it
is justice itself, after all, that we are seeking by means of
these and any other techniques that are humanly acceptable. Are there not instances when freedom and the
existing system of justice must be actively fought for,
or lost altogether, such as prior to the American Civil
War and World War II, where failure to act in any way
short of violence would have proved fatal to the cause
of human justice? Rather than an absolute value in itself, nonviolence is but one of many closely related
values which humanitarian people share; the desirability of one value, be it peace or social justice, must be
placed in the balance and weighed along with others.

In itself, the doctrine of nonviolence is an empty for-
malism: its logic does not inform concrete cases. To state
that one should do good and avoid evil is not to be told

how that injunction translates into concrete behavior. Both the capacity for deciding what is good and affirming the existence of conscience as a separate faculty, as King has done, call for an ethical intuition or some form of nonrational cognition which in everyone, obviously, is not developed to the same degree. It is easy to see how such a position can lead to self-righteousness, simply from a failure to realize that motives are commonly a mixture of right and wrong, of selfishness and disinterest, of responsibility and irresponsibility. Self-righteousness stems from a notion that one has a monopoly on what is good, an attitude that can lead to the vilest acts committed in the name of good. By uncritically assuming that his way is *the* right way it is difficult to see how the practice of nonviolence could lead a person to overcoming his faults. When, however, we elect to participate nonviolently with the knowledge that we are involved in the full consequences of an existential risk, then our stance is no longer absolute and our practice can be a learning and adaptive one.

An Indian critic, comparing King's uses of nonviolence to Gandhi's, pointed to their common flare for arranging demonstrations as if they were artistic performances. Art, rather than economics, theology, and politics was the essence of the nonviolent movement, as observed by Ved Metha.[14] It is the latter's thesis that when this century closes Gandhi and his followers will be counted as very influential men, but not because of their religious beliefs, and not even because of their political successes, but because "they were imaginative artists who knew how to use world politics as their stage."[15] Here, no one can dispute that King's oratorical skill and the "faith acts" he called upon when leading nonviolent demonstrations did, indeed, show artistry in their employment of rhetorical as well as nonviolent techniques.

A sense of the moral and historic dimensions of an act, the ability to project its reality into mythic drama, these were indispensable for involving the imagination of masses of men. But it is the essential character of myth, elements of which can be found in all social movements, to stir men emotionally rather than by practical or scientific demonstration. The profound social consequences which may result from myths which project even the most unattainable and ideal futures are not to be underestimated. Though they may fall far short of their goals, social myths may shape the direction of men's thoughts and behavior for long periods of time.

Christianity offers a prime example of myth and doctrine that has altered the course of Western civilization and profoundly influenced the attitudes of millions without having come close to realizing on earth its millennial aspirations. The dream of sixteenth-century reformers of a Europe religiously regenerated, set in motion radical changes in the relationship between church and state, as well as between men and God, without approximating the spiritual transformation aimed at by its initiators. And so too, King's call to nonviolent action must be regarded in terms not only of a moral philosophy but of a tremendously appealing social myth with the power to effect broad and significant changes.

Considering the higher degree of relevance usually enjoyed by social myths on their own cultural soil, we might ask whether the technique of nonviolence, as it was first used by Gandhi, is the one best suited to solving problems in Western society, and the problems of black people particularly. As pointed out by Nathan Hare, blacks have never participated in a nonviolent demonstration under attack. To do so, Hare insists, would be, in the light of the American tradition of violence, most unnatural. The "socialization" of black men to conditions of violence does not make nonviolence an emotionally true or appropriate response, especially in those areas where the unpunished killing of a black man is a not uncommon occurrence.[16] King made the dangerous assumption that religious experience would suffice to cancel out the tendency to resort to violence under any and all circumstances and within an environment notorious for its irrational violence. Is the continual sublimation of violent impulses which nonviolence calls for not an unrealistic, possibly even an unhealthy demand? The continual humiliation and threats to which nonviolent resisters are exposed make them particularly susceptible to intense feelings of anger and revenge—the very kinds of feelings they must be most careful to avoid. And, if these feelings continue to be denied expression, where are they eventually to find release? A safe conclusion would be that no single form of waging battle or dealing with conflict is guaranteed always to win. The most one can say is that where nonviolent techniques have failed, as they did at Albany, Georgia, violent methods would have proven even more disastrous. The most distinctive merit in nonviolence may simply be in the fact that in most instances it provokes less violence than its opposite.

And, finally, can a concept of nonviolence based on an individual morality, bred in situations of interpersonal relationships, in notions of love (agape), and expressed in canons of religious belief and moral behavior, can these values be transferred intact and undiminished to the political arena, the arena of the mass society, of collective behavior, or public decision-making? Isn't it necessary to distinguish clearly the moral and social behavior of groups from the moral and social behavior of individuals? The moral advantages of nonviolence for the individual in his personal relationships may be perfectly obvious, but the merits of this same pattern of behavior might well be lost in a larger, more complex social context.

Philosophical considerations apart, from a purely pragmatic standpoint, black power theorists have attacked King's social analysis and his strategy broadside. By arguing that violence is as American as cherry pie and that nonviolence is foreign to the American grain, some have loudly advocated violence as the only appropriate means for achieving racial justice. To pretend otherwise would be equal to calling upon black men to contradict their own basic, natural, and, by implication, "healthy" tendencies.[17]

Drawing from Fanon's *The Wretched of the Earth* and Sorel's *Reflections on Violence,* black power theorists argue that violence is a "psychologically healthy and tactically sound method for the oppressed." Only through violence can blacks achieve liberation and cleanse themselves of inferiority and the sin of submission which, in their eyes, nonviolence so much resembles. For, to refuse to defend oneself is the same as to submit.

King replied to these arguments by stating that "the line between defensive violence and aggressive or retaliatory violence is a fine line indeed."[18] In sum, retaliatory violence in King's view—even when justifiable —would cause blacks to lose the moral edge provided by nonviolence and to sink to the level of the oppressors.

On this point his estimation never altered; he remained convinced that "for practical as well as moral reasons, nonviolence offers the only road to freedom for my people."

But neither King nor the black power advocates solved the problem of nonviolence versus violence. Each side enunciated the virtues and validity of its choice of tactic without completely disproving the arguments of the other. Throughout history proponents of violence and of nonviolence have brought forth opposing arguments backed by reasons and examples that would amply justify their stand.[19] But whether either side has the exclusive prerogative of being right is doubtful. To insist under all circumstances upon the use of one and only one tactic is to become dogmatic and unrealistic, to treat political means as an historical absolute. The legacy of violence is with us, and King as well as the black power theorists have heightened the ancient debate without bringing it as yet to a successful compromise or conclusion.

In addition to attacking the wisdom of nonviolence, black power advocates have turned their backs on King's advocacy of alliances and coalitions, especially those between blacks and whites.[20] Black power militants point to the record of the past three hundred years as evidence that coalitions have failed utterly to achieve justice or equality. The reason for this failure they attribute to the numerous betrayals of blacks within these alliances.[21] Whites, they contend, have taken advantage of the lack of unity and solidarity in the black community and used it to promote themselves at the expense of blacks. Blacks, in their view, have been sold out time and again, whereas whites have constantly reaped the benefits of all coalition. Thus, for black militants, coalition politics are dead for the reason that whites are without scruple or principles. Likewise, they argue, morality has little place in American society where the struggle between conflicting interest groups is constantly being waged. An appeal to conscience is irrelevant, because power is the key, not love and not virtue. Power, not morality, is what decides issues and creates change. Without power little of consequence can be accomplished.

It follows that the first task of the black community is to close ranks and establish its own power base before entering into alliances with white society. This holding back further protects black society from contaminating contact with the degeneracy of white elements. Blacks frequently are viewed as a highly moral, innately good people with a mission to accomplish.[22] Any interaction with lesser beings, i.e. whites, could have a negative influence on their character. Thus on both practical and moral grounds, many black power advocates shun coalitions with the dominant society.

In this respect King's position was far less inflexible than many, for he thought every alliance should be considered on its own merits. Recognizing that the pluralistic structure of our society creates the need for coalition, he counseled blacks to accept some and reject others.[23] Since strength or power grows through amalgamation, and because black and white alliances proved constructive in the past, King regarded continued cooperation necessary to social progress. To the charge that association with their "inferiors" might prove harmful to Negroes, King made no reply.

Yet the problem of creating meaningful, fruitful, cooperative coalitions between blacks and whites was not carried any closer to a solution through King's dialogue with black power advocates. While the latter refused to acknowledge the strength that could come from some alliances, King neglected to set forth a basis by which to judge coalition arrangements.

Basically, the antagonism between the position of black power advocates and King lies in their divergent visions of what, ultimately, is socially desirable for the black community: black separatism or an integrated state wherein all races would be as brothers. Rather than shun the white man for his fallen state, King saw his redemption to be the particular province of the black mission. On this score he saw black militants as having given up on one of the crucial tasks, of having forsaken one of their duties toward God. For only through complete integration could the unity and essence of the beloved community be expressed, and that was the final vision toward which all other activity aimed.

Another area of King's political philosophy which leaves us with many questions unanswered is that of the individual's relationship to civil disobedience. King concluded that one has a moral duty as well as a civic obligation to obey just laws and disobey unjust ones. However, to prevent society from being engulfed in chaos he stressed that if one does disobey unjust laws he must willingly accept the penalty imposed under law. But is this simple formulation adequate to prevent society from degenerating into chaos and disrespect for the law? If individual conscience is to be the arbiter of whether or not the law is obeyed, is allegiance then not owing solely to one's personal God and none to the state? Could law and order prevail if such a view were to predominate? The question of political obligation to the state versus individual rights has been of concern to political theorists since the time of Socrates. A brief review of some of the arguments and formulations of this problem might here be in order.

A classic formulation was made by Thomas Hill Green in 1879–1880 when he asserted that government and political institutions are to be judged by the extent to which they contribute to the development of the individual citizen.[24] For a man to live a life he could call his own he must be free to work toward self-perfection, and it is this freedom of action that is the function of law to preserve. By men acting as members of a social organization in which each freely contributes to the well-being of the rest, a cohesive will is generated which then both creates and sustains the state.[25] By giving his obedience to the state—which has as its aim the highest development of every member—each man can attain to his highest perfection.

Other political theorists, before and after Green, reflecting on the same subject reached very different conclusions. It was G. W. F. Hegel's thesis that man must submit to the state because it was thus ordained by God: to disobey the state was to disobey God.[26] Men like Thomas Hobbes and John Dickinson proclaimed a near absolutism based not upon identification of the state with God but with an absolute sovereign whose laws, if disobeyed, would severely undermine the power of the state and lead to destructive anarchy.[27] At the opposite pole, thinkers such as H. J. Laski,[28] Thoreau, and Gandhi have advocated an extreme type of individualism vis-à-vis the state, contending that final obedience is to the conscience of the individual rather than to any political order.

As with other aspects of the relationship between individuals and society, King viewed the question of political obligation as essentially a moral concern. When the laws of the state are found to be conflicting with the law of God, then civil disobedience is the duty of every righteous man. Cognizant of the damage that could be done the social order if civil disobedience should degenerate to criminal law-breaking, or such acts be committed in the name of a higher cause, King upheld the state's right to punish those who resisted its edicts, concluding that its penalties should be manfully met by all nonviolent civil resisters. Where civil resisters abide by the law it should not be out of fear of punishment but because those laws are deemed good for the general social welfare. If a law is so unjust as to offend one's moral sense and if all efforts to have it modified fail, King advocated taking a public stand against that law and calmly accepting the consequences for such a stand. Looked at this way, civil disobedience, though aimed at destroying immoral laws and an unjust order, neither creates lawlessness nor is it unprogressive.

True, such a stand might be regarded as no more than a token form of civil disobedience, falling far short of jeopardizing the economy or bringing society to a halt, as some of the collective acts of civil disobedience organized by Gandhi managed to do. Black historian Lerone Bennett, Jr. asserts that King was not quite sure that the moment had come for a full-scale civil disobedience campaign. But that possibility was in the air in the mid-sixties, making it easy to envisage a day when all the transportation centers would be filled by masses of civil resisters, nonviolently insisting on "freedom now." But for King the painful delays and slow results yielded enough of change and the hope for change to avoid the call for an all-out civil disobedience campaign. Throughout his writings, he stayed with the concept of individual civil disobedience as a morally significant symbolic act. Nor, for that matter, was his organization in a position to conduct a nationwide civil disobedience campaign that would be coherent and meaningful.

King's facile acceptance of the punishment meted out by the state for the infringement of its laws not only neglects to examine whether and by what standard that punishment is itself just, it implies carte blanche acceptance of the juridical process, which, at this point in our national experience, bespeaks a tremendous naivete. We are told that a just law is one in harmony with the law of God, but might not different men have different and conflicting concepts of God's just laws? Don't the segregationists, just as surely as those who oppose them, believe that God is on their side? What one man believes to be an act of conscience may, indeed, do another a grave injustice. Confounded with a variety of interpretations all claiming the sanction of God's law, is it not conceivable that no one nor all of them together may do justice to God's law?

We can see that King's appeal to individual conscience as a solution to the problem of political allegiance is based on circular reasoning, simple in its moral categories, but not very convincing or useful when up against the brute facts of social reality. But it is no easy task to formulate a criteria for deciding the justness of laws. The right, if not the obligation to commit acts of civil disobedience, and the demand for an orderly society has been, and still is, an issue of considerable controversy for which there seems to be no single, definitive answer. A strong case can be made both for civil disobedience and for obedience to the state.[29]

Having looked at King's recommendations for attacking social injustice, especially segregation, and found them somewhat wanting, we might look to his proposals for the building of a new political base for the black community.

Like black thinkers before him, King advocated measures of self-help and the formation of black alliances with organized labor, insisting that the fate of the two were intimately linked. What he seems to have overlooked here is the threat of backlash from such a relationship, the fear of many upper-class whites of any alliance which might by uniting join forces against them. In a competitive economic system it is not uncommon for employers to play off one group against another; to follow the time-tested formula of divide and rule. Therefore, while an alliance with labor could help rid the black man of some of the economic deprivation caused by discrimination, it could equally harm him by arousing in his fellow white workers the fear of economic competition, and in the upper classes the fear of lower-class consolidation.

King also argued for strong governmental action and leadership by the Chief Executive on behalf of minorities, but it is not always feasible for either the President or Congress to address itself to the domestic scene. Other problems of like magnitude plague the government, often claiming priority. King realized that in a time of national crisis and tension the needs of minorities are forgotten,[30] and he called upon blacks to relax their efforts and demands at those times.

To ask, as King did, that the blacks form voting blocs and vote in accordance with the party most favorable to their interests, is to expect a great degree of political coordination and cooperation from them. Whether they possess at this point the requisite sophistication and agreement for this kind of group action is highly doubtful. Since the reforms of the New Deal blacks have largely aligned with the Democratic party and, given the relative status of the social and economic conditions of the majority of blacks, a change in their voting loyalty can be safely precluded. It seems also safe to predict that Negroes will remain a disruptive force politically.[31]

Crucial to the problem of forming voting blocs amongst the black community is the tremendous weight of social conditioning separating not only blacks from the North and South, but the thinking of different economic segments within the same region. These complex and extremely important factors King totally overlooks, or bypasses as self-annealing.

One would expect any concerted political movement to recognize the need to adapt to regional differences if it hoped to rally people and involve them in its strategies. The differences in the ways segregation is expressed in the South where it is flagrant and clearly targeted and in the North where it is often subtle and indirect, raise the question whether nonviolent action is well-suited to countering the more devious forms of northern discrimination. The kind of situation where it did prove applicable was in the selective buying campaign organized in Philadelphia and in other boycotts and sit-ins. However, a strategy of "love" employed against school segregation or discrimination in employment and housing is hardly likely to have equally clearcut results. The added fact that in the North the identity of the oppressor is frequently unknown, makes it especially difficult to extend him love. To uncritically pursue the strategies of King's nonviolent ethic wherever political action was called for, would seem, in some cases, a willful act of political suicide.

While on the surface King's thought seems to reflect

a certain healthiness and stability of attitude, deeper analysis has led psychologist Kenneth Clark to refer to an "unrealistic, if not pathological basis in . . . his doctrine."[32] Clark also points out the additional and intolerable psychological burden upon the oppressed if it is demanded that he love his oppressor. The natural human reaction to humiliation and degradation is resentment and bitterness, not love. In answer to criticisms of this kind, King called attention to the fact that a proper interpretation of his philosophy of love and nonviolence must take into account its Christian origins and significance, a feat, however, for which but a minority of educated individuals are equipped, provided they had the interest. If Clark is right, the reason for widespread acceptance of King's philosophy among liberal and moderate whites is that it is consistent with the stereotype of the black man as long-suffering, meek, and more apt to resort to prayer than take decisive action against injustice.[33] These accusations were never directly countered in King's writings: instead he appears to have brushed them aside as either irrelevant or unimportant in the framework of his mind.

Other questions arise with regard to the attempt to fuse into a political philosophy elements from sources as diverse as Gandhi, Thoreau, and Jesus. Does King's attempt at a unifying theory hold up under close scrutiny, or does the amalgam prove tenuous, a forced synthesis of basically dissimilar religious ideals? It has been suggested by the black theologian, Joseph R. Washington, Jr., that from Gandhi King borrowed nonviolence and a syncretic spirit which, through the persuasive force of his personality, blacks were then led to accept, mistaking religion for faith. The risk in any syncreticism is that it overlooks the contradictions between different religious faiths. In King's endeavor to combine nonviolence with Christian love what we see is systematic theology being subordinated to a political philosophy.[34] It is precisely this attempt to reconcile the doctrines of various philosophers that accounts for what in King's position remains vague, highly ambiguous, and abstract, sometimes to the point of seeming utterly unrealistic.

King's attempt to bring together the highest kind of religious idealism with sound, practical methodology resulted in an insistence on the coming into being of a purely utopian community, a just society which, if it ever were to be attained, would require a much greater transformation than any ever envisioned even by King. The gap between the ideal envisaged and the reality at hand is much too ponderous to be bridged by powerful convictions. In contrast to the harmony one might like to believe pervades the entire universe and with it all of our existences, there are also enormous gulfs, deep disagreements, and cross purposes.

His formula for a harmonization of political actions, calling for "a rhythmic alteration between attacking the causes and healing the effects" does not, whatever its aesthetic appeal, tell us what we need to know. In many instances there is no real relationship between what appears to be a cause and what appears to be an effect. Or, what may seem causal may, on further analysis, be equally regarded as an effect, and vice versa. Given the arbitrariness of any line between cause and effect, where then is the harmonizing balance to be struck between them?

In view of the many questions raised by King's political philosophy in its attempt to synthesize disparate elements into a single vision having universal appeal and moral force, what conclusions can be drawn?

NOTES

1. Washington, Jr., *Black Religion*, p. 8.
2. Niebuhr, *The Nature and Destiny of Man*, vol. 1, p. 73.
3. Ibid.
4. Ibid., pp. 73–74.
5. Ibid., p. 170.
6. Miller, *Non-Violence*, p. 33.
7. Smith, "A Strange Kind of Love," p. 19.
8. Bennett, *What Manner of Man*, p. 206.
9. King, *Why We Can't Wait*, pp. 90–91.
10. H. L. Nieburg, "The Threat of Violence and Social Change" and "Uses of Violence."
11. Niebuhr, *Moral Man and Immoral Society*, p. 240.
12. King, *Why We Can't Wait*, pp. 88–89.
13. Zinn, "The Force of Nonviolence," p. 229.
14. Metha, "Gandhism Is Not Easily Copied."
15. Ibid.
16. Hare, "An Epitaph for Nonviolence."
17. There is no one book that clearly defines all of the ideas associated with black power, but many books on the subject. Some which advance the thesis of violence as a tool for racial justice are those by Barbour, ed.; Carmichael and Hamilton; Wagstaff, ed.; and Stokely Carmichael's Black Power "Position Paper."
18. King, "Nonviolence: The Only Road to Freedom."
19. See Fanon, *The Wretched of the Earth*; Sorel, *Reflections on Violence*; Coser, "Some Social Functions of Violence."
20. Carmichael and Hamilton, *Black Power*, pp. 58–85.
21. Ibid., pp. 86–97.
22. Fullinwider, *The Mind and Mood of Black America*, pp. 241–248.
23. King, *Where Do We Go From Here*, p. 51.
24. Green, *Lectures on the Principle of Political Obligation*, pp. 9–87; see also Plamenatz, *Consent, Freedom and Political Obligation*, chap. 1–4, and Barker, *Principles of Social and Political Theory*, vol. 6.
25. David Spitz, "Democracy and the Problem of Civil Disobedience," p. 399; see also: Christian Bay, "Civil Disobedience:

Prerequisite for Democracy in Mass Society," in Spitz's *Political Theory and Social Change* (New York: Atherton Press, 1967), pp. 163–182; and Michael Walzer, "The Obligation to Disobey," in the same volume, pp. 185–201.

26. Hegel, *Phenomonology of Mind,* vol. 2, p. 453.

27. Dickinson, "A Working Theory of Sovereignty."

28. Laski, *Authority in the Modern State,* pp. 43–46.

29. Spitz, "Democracy and the Problem of Civil Disobedience," p. 348; see also his *Patterns of Anti-Democratic Thought,* pp. 204–206, 247–248, and *Democracy and the Challenge of Power,* pp. 4–200. Also, Hugh A. Bedau, ed., *Civil Disobedience: Theory and Practice* (New York: Pegasus, 1969).

30. King, "Fumbling on the New Frontier," p. 90.

31. Lubell, *White and Black,* pp. 170–172. For additional black political strategies see Hanes Walton, Jr., *The Negro in Third Party Politics* (Philadelphia: Dorrance, 1969) and his *Black Political Parties* (New York: Free Press, 1970).

32. Kenneth B. Clark, "The New Negro in the North," in Ahmann, ed., *The New Negro,* p. 36.

33. Ibid., p. 37.

34. Washington, Jr., *Black Religion,* pp. 9–10.

5 | Summary and Conclusions

THE EMOTIONAL basis of King's political thought was rooted in the black man's struggle for equality and social justice in America, a struggle whose progress has always greatly depended upon the power of ideas, theories, and persuasive arguments. His development of nonviolent civil disobedience provided the black movement with a new impetus and carried it to new heights. It won for blacks many victories in civil rights; it helped the black movement generally in its struggle for greater social justice and equality; and finally, it has helped to imbue the black man with a new sense of dignity and personal worth.

The concepts of nonviolence and civil disobedience were drawn from the past where they had been consistently used by weak groups imbedded in a strong religious tradition, and with little hope of gaining their ends by violent means. King conceded that it was the strong black religious tradition which made his philosophy of nonviolence a living reality.[1] But it was not until after the northern riots in the summer of 1964 that he realized the entire black community did not fully accept the philosophy of nonviolence.[2] What religious influence that may once have predominated in blacks originally from the South was no longer a major force. After the Watts riot of 1965, King stated publicly that the black communities everywhere would accept the philosophy of nonviolence. Yet he claimed that black adherence to nonviolence could not be taken for granted, and that rage rather than reason is present when rocklike intransigence or sophisticated manipulation makes mockery of a parishioner.[3] In an unpublished article, King admitted that his movement had been essentially regional, not national, and that the solutions, issues, and changes were also regional and only affected a certain area.[4] Regardless of the riots and seemingly inoperative religious tradition in some areas, King still felt that the entire black community would come to embrace his philosophy of nonviolence.[5] He felt that in areas like the North, "the critical task will be to convince Negroes driven to cynicism that nonviolence can win."[6] And he was confident that the majority of blacks, North and South, would eventually embrace nonviolence.[7] Admitting that the sophisticated northern black man might be reluctant to embrace the "moral simplicities" of nonviolence, King nonetheless thought that he would finally be forced to adopt it on tactical grounds,[8] so convinced was he that nonviolence was the only moral and potent weapon available to oppressed people.

As we find in the history of political nonviolence the primary ideas underlining King's position, we also find in it a tradition whose proponents have adhered tenaciously to the fundaments of their moral beliefs. King was no exception. He continued to insist upon the efficacy of nonviolence even when the very people who were supposed to be accepting it were, in fact, repudiating it. For earlier champions of nonviolence it was a way of life and the only way.

The chief tribute that can be paid King's political philosophy is that it accomplished in civil rights what no amount of theorizing or activism alone had been able to. Despite its weaknesses as a political philosophy, and its abrupt uselessness in the black ghettoes, it helped redress the balance of relationships between men of different races. It also provided motive and justification for a black movement in this country. Race relations in America—after the impact of King's philosophy—were never quite the same. Whether the dismantling of southern segregation practices would have occurred by some other means is beside the point. The fact is that change did not begin to occur until King arrived. To be sure, the black man's burden was not suddenly removed, his problems solved, and his place in the beloved community assured. But the old order was left in a shambles; southern segregation and relations between blacks and whites entered the American consciousness with a force that will not easily permit their repression.

If Locke provided the British colonials in America with a reason sufficient for revolution, and if Marx has given the proletariat something to look forward to, King gave blacks a philosophical method with which to reconstruct the southern racist society which was constructed during the three decades after 1877. His philosophy, in combination with his leadership, gave the black masses what black thinkers from the time of Reconstruction until 1955 had not been able to give them—a tool for removing the invisible shades of segregation. And, although his method proved less useful in the North than in the South, it was useful nevertheless.

Despite the philosophical shortcomings in King's political thought, its logical inconsistencies, moral idealism, and inherent biases, it is not easily discarded. Other political philosophers have had similar difficulties: Plato's political philosophy suffered from an inherent utopian stance; Locke took for granted the existence of natural law, and Marx was limited by a monistic interpretation of history. More important than these limitations may be that each philosopher gave a fresh approach, a new intellectual tool, a vision, and a definite point of view, the consequences of which are not to be ascertained by logical analyses, though from that too we may learn new ways of perceiving and structuring the future as well as the past.

Paradoxically, it is in those very elements which largely accounted for the success of King's philosophy, in nonviolence and civil disobedience, that we also find its chief weaknesses. Not philosophic perfection, but the emotional and spiritual appeal of nonviolence were crucial in deciding whether it was to be ignored or accepted; a fate King's philosophy shares, in the end, with the fate of all others. The doctrine of natural law was taken up largely because it provided the necessary rational basis for the colonies to revolt against England, arguing that their natural rights were being infringed upon. The persistent attraction of Marx's economic interpretation of history relies upon the emotional outrage of a great many "have nots" and those sensitive to the injustice of that condition, more than it does upon its adequacy in accounting for the complex web of historical motivation. Similarly, the forces stirred by King's philosophy were quite independent of its purely intellectual validity.

The starting point of King's philosophy, as well as his final vision, was basically religious, dependent upon his faith in God and in the power of love to transform the hearts and minds of men. These two great forces were seen as responsible for holding together the universe, and as being continually manifest throughout the unity of creation. From this perception of spiritual unity,

King's entire philosophy is derived. Man, rooted in God, depends for his growth and self-expression on his relationship to God. The greatest good is the unity of all life, and self-fulfillment consists in helping and serving the whole of mankind. Loving service toward all is nonviolence. Thus, God can be pursued only by nonviolent means. As a corollary, King insisted that to achieve the greatest good for all, the means must be as pure as the end, and there must be no dual ethical code for individual and group conduct.

The greatest good toward which mankind is consciously or unconsciously striving will be achieved when individual and social life are imbued with God-like qualities. These require the exercise of self-control, which is acquired by the pursuit of nonviolent values. Violence, King asserted, offends not only God, but the unity and sacredness of all life. Nonviolence means the highest possible love, agape, which seeks to overcome evil with truth, to resist physical force by soul-force, and to convert the evildoer by an act of creative suffering. Since the object of all striving is the pursuit of God through nonviolent means, King wanted to effect a revalorization of current values directed toward a life of inner harmony.

Nonviolence in both its constructive and its cleansing aspects is the instrument of social progress in King's philosophy. Constructive nonviolence develops the moral strength of the people and disciplines them for the use of nonviolent direct action, which is the sole technique for transforming the existing social order along moral lines into one that will be stable and lasting. As a method of resisting injustice and settling conflicts, nonviolence is an excellent technique. The nonviolent resister aims at bringing about a change of heart in his opponent and awakening in him a sense of justice. If appeals to reason fail, the nonviolent resister then tries through creative suffering to reach his opponent. King did not envisage the elimination of all conflict, but aimed at raising conflict from the destructive physical plane to the constructive moral plane where differences could be peacefully adjusted and antagonisms, rather than antagonists, liquidated.

According to King's philosophy, nonviolence integrates legitimate differences instead of suppressing them; its gains, therefore, are likely to be stable and permanent, and the risk of counter-revolution minimal. By the exercise of soul-force, nonviolent resistance achieves the approximation of the social order to the moral order. Through nonviolence a cooperative social order based on justice and nonviolence may come into being and the unjust system based on exploitation be extinguished. The belief that all men have infinite moral worth means that they should be treated as ends in themselves and not as means. Nonviolence alone is the democratic technique which can lead to the establishment of the beloved community.

Thus, King's political philosophy was an organic part of his philosophy of life. For him the isolation of politics from moral principles was a serious error. He saw the method of nonviolent resistance as a great contribution to the philosophy and techniques of revolution, a way of restoring morality to politics. His attempts to show how a racial minority within a democracy can resist immoral laws and unjust institutions nonviolently, and acquire the maximum amount of consideration, are not to be dismissed lightly, however much his proposals for attacking the roots of injustice left to be desired. King claimed for his approach that it answered the problem of immediacy versus gradualism, insofar as it recognizes that social change does not occur overnight, while, at the same time, to retard justice is immoral. Another virtue of nonviolence is that it saves one from hasty judgment and irresponsible words, and, finally, it combats passive acquiescence to oppression.

One can readily see that King claims too much for the nonviolent method. No single political technique can possess such all-embracing virtues. Some situations may call for a more gradual approach, others for "freedom now." Nonviolence is one technique among many; it may cause fewer casualties than another, but this does not give it supreme virtue. No amount of theological rationalization can make nonviolence any more or less moral than it is. Theology can only *ascribe* morality to nonviolence, and this is exactly what King has done. He has used theology to enhance the moral status of nonviolence and to explain how it is morally superior to any other method.[9]

Analysis of King's reasoning shows that the whole subject of nonviolence and civil disobedience is a delicate one which the moralist and the political scientist must approach with clear concepts, exact definitions, and close reasoning. The facts of social and political life are, unfortunately, such as to make the use of some violence necessary, under certain circumstances, in order to achieve an objective the nonachievement of which would constitute a greater evil than that involved in the use of violence. But the need for violence is just as regrettable as the existence of those facts which may necessitate it, and any exaltation or joy in its use is a definite perversity.

Is violence always relatively inefficient, as King has declared? Obviously not for those amoral enough to wholly adapt it to an evil design. But is violence used for a worthy end always less effective than nonviolence would be under the same circumstances? A worthy cause could mean self-defense or effecting some positive reform. If a man attacks another with definite intent to kill, the person assailed is hardly likely to doubt the relative efficacy of a pistol to that of passive resistance. In such a case, violence would be the only "efficient" means for defending an individual life. Most men will readily be able to imagine situations in which the defense of an individual or a group requires the use of violence.

In the realm of what King called large-scale social reforms the utility of violence is not so evident. The fact, upon which he laid so much emphasis, that violence cannot lead to real progress unless it is followed by compensatory acts of nonviolence, does not in itself prove that violence is never necessary. It simply means that by itself violence is not enough; it may, however, be an indispensable prerequisite to progress. It is true that the use of violence is potentially dangerous, for a habit of violent recourse may easily be formed—all too often violence begets violence. But the possibility of abuse does not automatically preclude a rightful use; an equally effective way to achieve the same results must be found before it can be said that violence should never be employed.

Discussion of the pros and cons of the relative values of violence and nonviolence could continue almost indefinitely. What is important here to an understanding of King's position is that it was not based primarily on the effective superiority of nonviolence over violence—though he held to that too—but on its moral preferability, its concordance with the larger unity of being in which all men and all phenomena participate.

But, whatever the name given a philosophy which supposes the fundamental unity of all being, it is open to the same criticism as any monistic formulation of reality. A discussion of the metaphysical difficulties of monism—in King's philosophy a pantheistic monism—and its negative implications for ethics shall not be gone into here: that work has been ably accomplished by others.[10] Suffice it to say that a study of the history of philosophy will show that any positive ethical theory in monistic systems derives from extraneous concepts, often basically incompatible with monism or representing a deviation from or modification of pure monism. It is in this respect that King's thought seems most detached from concrete awareness; for the mere realization of unity has no significance unless interpreted in terms which give that unity value. Knowing that we are made of the same essential substance as rocks will not make us love men. The basis of love for our fellow men is not an abstract identity of being, but realization of our common human nature sharing a common and higher ethical purpose.

The argument that we must practice morality to achieve unity with ultimate reality leads not to the realization of an ultimate reality lying outside of individual perceptions, but to a logical impasse which either develops into nihilism, the introduction of personal and ethical deities, or a reversion to absolute nonviolence.[11]

Also curiously overlooked by King in his concerted attention to the problem of ethical group action, was the ethical dilemma of the individual faced, for example, with an imminent threat to his life. Nowhere does the uncompromising advocate of nonviolence touch upon its use in relations between individuals. It should be remarked, however, that ordinary people, as well as those of exceptional moral force, have, when strengthened by intense convictions, frequently demonstrated great power to overcome tremendous obstacles and physical danger by nonviolent means.

Another point on which King was silent was the right of the state to employ violence in carrying out its lawful functions. This function can only conceivably be justified in a democratic state when the use of force is coordinated to an end the achievement of which is a legitimate function of the state. Hence, any attempt to establish the moral authority of the state must begin with a clear understanding and acceptance of its overall purpose by the citizenry. From a moralist's point of view, the use of violence by the state in law enforcement is justifiable because it is necessary to fulfill the functions of the state. But state violence is inherently no more justifiable than individual violence exerted in defense of a personal right. When we are faced in our time with the overwhelming deployment of violence by the state, from one end of the scale to the other, the failure of King to comment on this is a major deficiency in the writings of a man primarily concerned with the moral issues of political behavior.

What we find is that King's advocacy of nonviolence derives not from a basic philosophy of value, but reveals a cleavage between social and political values. While able to present a strong case for the relative efficacy of nonviolence, he was unable to prove that it is under all circumstances the only acceptable means. When faced with the state's recourse to violence, his position, if only by omission, seems to waver.

In the absence of fuller discussion of the subject, it would be a mistake to imagine that violence plays a more positive role in the regulation of our collective life than it actually does or can. Compulsion, which always carries the threat of violence, can never be a good thing; at best, it may involve no moral wrong. But its use always involves some privation of a good which, as the metaphysicians say, is what constitutes evil in the ontological order.[12] From the ontological point of view, the situation of an imprisoned criminal is just as evil as that of a man stranded on a desert island after a shipwreck, since both suffer from a privation of freedom which is a right owing to humans. Physical violence in any form involves evil or potential evil in its toll of death, discomfort, or restriction of movement. Only to prevent the advent of an otherwise inevitable evil, physical or moral, is the use of violence at all justifiable.

Now that we have looked at King's solutions for attacking what he considered to be the causes of injustice, let us turn to his remedies for the effects of minority deprivation. These, in the main, are a recombination of the proposals of earlier black thinkers. Black economic self-help recalls Booker T. Washington's efforts on behalf of small black businessmen; proposals for labor alliances echo A. Philip Randolph; the call for voting blocs and political alliances bring to mind Du Bois' early theories; the willingness to rely on the courts and legal procedures is closely allied to the NAACP approach, and his concept of inner transformation accompanied by political protest harks back to Fredrick Douglass' ideas. To have resuscitated the proposals of others is in itself no deficiency. On the contrary we find in the past a rich store of ingenious theoretical solutions to problems that are still with us. What is missing is a unified approach, a program for adapting these various proposals concurrently, so that they might be meaningfully applied.

If love was to act as the universal lubricant catalyzing social transformation on all fronts, then we have only to look at the examples of Montgomery and Selma, towns that have undergone a nonviolent struggle and serve as concrete illustrations that love has surely not created a climate of reconciliation or healed the broken community. Both communities remain fragmented and divided. Love, it would seem, needs not only to be given voluntarily, but needs also to be a two-way process if it is to transform human relations.

In summation, King's political thought is revealed on analysis to be fragmentary and lacking in systematic order and, therefore, not completely convincing. Repetition, and like any master orator King was repetitious, is no substitute for the substance of thought. He overestimated the good in human nature and underestimated human egoism and self-interest. In his absolutizing of God and nonviolence, King converted moral ideas into a political theology, in the sense that these moral values are based on divine revelation and belief in God. From these revelations certain principles and "laws" were ascertained which became the foundation for the development of King's political theories.

By theology is not meant what Aristotle called theology, i.e., the inquiry into divine things, as distinguished from the account of divine things given by mythographers, poets, legislators, and the ancestral tradition. Theology in the present context derives from the distinction made by the medieval scholastics between natural and sacred theology, the latter being an inquiry into divine things based upon divine revelation, the highest principles of which are not accessible to the unassisted human mind. Thus, political theology is the elucidation of political teachings given through divine revelation, or the inquiry into political subjects based on the moral implications of divine revelation.[13]

In one sense King's political theory can be conceived of as more comprehensive than ordinary political philosophy because, according to King, it saw further and more deeply into the nature of human community. It asks whether we do not need something more, a higher knowledge than that offered by political philosophy. King was personally convinced that the precepts of the divine law and the beliefs prescribed by it are the only path to salvation, and that no other law and no other kind of knowledge is sufficient for this purpose. The multiplicity of laws—man-made and divine—did not disturb him; he simply rejected those he found false or incomplete. He was absolute in his belief that he must follow his own divine law and no other, and that his divine law goes beyond all the precepts of a merely human science. King, a political theologian, was tied by the divine revelations and laws of his own particular social and religious community. Had he been first a political philosopher, he would have inquired into those matters which political theology unquestioningly accepts as its point of departure. More generally stated: the principles of political theology are the fundamentals of a particular religious polity. These fundamentals were revealed for the sake of that body and they constitute its basic belief. Political philosophy, on the other hand, is not bound to any particular religious or nonreligious polity. Whereas political theology examines the principles underlying a particular religious polity, political philosophy inquires into the principles and roots of all kinds of polities, without presupposing any articles of faith or beliefs. However, the seeming subordination of political theology to political philosophy here does not lessen the need for the former or diminish its importance as a social and moral discipline. It may be both necessary and useful for individual religious communities as well as a productive source of challenge to the concepts and values of the general political order.

The work of political theologians, particularly in the realm of moral philosophy, contributes to an area where mundane political life seems frequently most bankrupt. The error to which political theologians themselves are most liable—and this was certainly the case with King— is to try to extend revealed laws, or their interpretation of divine law, to all people and all situations. That we find King's political thought most directly applicable in those religious communities with a common background to his own, and increasingly less so as we move from those centers, comes as no surprise. Since man is both a political and a religious animal—and no less so when he makes of politics a religion—neither discipline can by itself claim to illumine fully all of what we may call political behavior. Both are needed.

NOTES

1. King, "The Burning Truth in the South." Prior to the rioting of 1964 King stated that it was the "religious tradition of Negroes" that made them fully accept nonviolence as a way of dealing with the white man.

2. King, "Next Stop: The North," pp. 35, 105.

3. Ibid., p. 35.

4. Ibid., p. 33.

5. Ibid., p. 35. See also King's *The Trumpet of Conscience,* pp. 53–66.

6. Ibid.

7. Ibid.

8. Ibid.

9. Alex Willingham, "The Religious Basis for Action in the Political Philosophy of Martin Luther King, Jr."

10. Coffey, *Ontology*, p. 46; Harnack, *What Is Christianity?*, p. 153; Joyce, *Principles of Natural Theology*, p. 481; Urquhart, *Pantheism and the Value of Life*.

11. Bennett, *What Manner of Man*, chap. 4.

12. Coffey, *Ontology*, p. 182.

13. Strauss, *What Is Political Philosophy*, pp. 12–22. See also Ralph Lerner and Muhsin Mahdi, eds., *Medieval Political Philosophy* (New York: Free Press, 1963).

Bibliography

Ahmann, M. H., ed. *The New Negro.* Notre Dame, Indiana: Fides Publisher, 1961.

American Society of African Culture, ed. *Pan-Africanism Reconsidered.* Berkeley: University of California Press, 1962.

Aptheker, Herbert. *A Documentary History of the Negro People in the United States.* New York: Citadel Press, 1951.

_____, ed. *One Continual Cry.* New York: Humanties Press, 1961.

Barbour, E. D., ed. *The Black Power Revolt.* Boston: Sargent Press, 1968.

Bardolph, Richard. *The Negro Vanguard.* New York: Vintage Books, 1961.

Barker, Ernest. *Principles of Social and Political Theory.* London: Oxford University Press, 1951.

Bell, Ingel P. *CORE and the Strategy of Nonviolence.* New York: Random House, 1968.

Bennett, Lerone. *Before the Mayflower.* Chicago: Johnson Publishing Co., 1962.

_____. *What Manner of Man.* Chicago: Johnson Publishing Co., 1964.

Blake, W. O. *The History of Slavery and the Slave Trade.* Columbus, Ohio: privately printed, 1861.

Bontemps, Arna, and Conroy, Jack. *Anyplace But Here.* New York: Hill and Wang, 1966.

Botkin, B. A., ed. *Lay My Burden Down: A Folk History of Slavery*. Chicago: University of Chicago Press, 1945.

Brandt, R. B. *Ethical Theory*. Englewood Cliffs, N. J.: Prentice-Hall, 1959.

Brawley, B. G. *A Short History of the American Negro*. New York: The Macmillan Co., 1939.

Brotz, Howard, ed. *Negro Social and Political Thought 1850–1920*. New York: Basic Books, 1966.

Brown, H. R. *Die Nigger Die*. New York: Dial Press, 1968.

Brunner, Emil. *Justice and the Social Order*. London: Butterworth Press, 1945.

Carmichael, S., and Hamilton, C. V. *Black Power*. New York: Random House, 1967.

Clark, K. B., ed. *The Negro Protest*. Boston: Beacon Press, 1963.

Clayton, Edward. *The Peaceful Warrior*. Englewood Cliffs, N.J.: Prentice-Hall, 1964.

Coffey, P. *Ontology*. London: Oxford University Press, 1914.

Coker, F. W. *Recent Political Thought*. New York: Appleton-Century-Crofts, 1934.

Davidson, Basil. *The Lost Cities of Africa*. Boston: Little, Brown Co., 1959.

Davis, John P., ed. *American Negro Reference Book*. Englewood Cliffs, N.J.: Prentice-Hall, 1966.

Fanon, Franz. *The Wretched of the Earth*. New York: Grove Press, 1963.

Fishel, Leslie H. *The Negro American: A Documentary History*. Glenview, Ill.: Scott, Foresman and Co., 1967.

Foner, Philip S., ed. *The Life and Writings of Frederick Douglass*. Vol. 2. New York: International Publishers, 1950.

Franklin, John H. *From Slavery to Freedom*. New York: Alfred Knopf, 1961.

Frazier, E. Franklin. *The Negro in the United States*. New York: The Macmillan Co., 1957.

Fullinwider, S. P. *The Mind and Mood of Black America:*

20 Century Thought. Homewood, Ill.: Dorsey Press, 1969.

Garfinkel, Herbert. *When Negroes March: The March on Washington Movement in the Organizational Politics for FEPC*. New York: Free Press, 1959.

Garvey, Amy, ed. *Philosophy and Opinion of Marcus Garvey*. New York: Universal Publishing House, 1923.

George, Henry. *Social Problems*. New York: Belford, Clarke and Co., 1883.

Gill, Theodore. *Recent Protestant Political Thought*. Privately printed, 1947.

Glazer, Nathan. *Beyond the Melting Pot*. Cambridge: M.I.T. Press, 1963.

Green, T. H. *Lectures on the Principle of Political Obligation*. London: Oxford University Press, 1924.

Grimes, Alan P. *American Political Thought*. New York: Holt, Rinehart & Winston, 1960.

Harnack, Adolph. *What Is Christianity?* London: George Bell & Sons, 1904.

Harris, R. J. *The Quest for Equality*. Baton Rouge: Louisiana State University Press, 1960.

Hegel, George W. F. *The Phenomenology of Mind*. Translated by J. B. Baillie. 2 vols. New York: T. C. Smith, 1910.

Hoffer, Eric. *The Ordeal of Change*. New York: Harper and Row, 1963.

Hospers, J. *Human Conduct*. New York: Harcourt, Brace and World, 1961.

Hughes, Langston. *Fight For Freedom: The Story of the NAACP*. New York: W. W. Norton & Co., 1962.

Hyneman, Charles S. *The Study of Politics*. Urbana: University of Illinois Press, 1959.

Jack, Robert L. *History of the National Association for the Advancement of Colored People*. Boston: Meador Publishing Co., 1943.

Jenkins, Thomas P. *The Study of Political Theory*. Garden City, N.J.: Doubleday and Co., 1955.

Jenkins, W. S. *Pro-Slavery Thought in the Old South.* Chapel Hill: University of North Carolina Press, 1935.

Jowett, B., trans. *The Dialogues of Plato.* Vol. I, 4th rev. ed. Oxford: Clarendon Press, 1964.

Joyce, George. *Principles of Natural Theology.* London: University Press, 1924.

Kellogg, Charles F. *NAACP: A History of the National Association for the Advancement of Colored People, 1909–1920.* Vol. I. Baltimore: Johns Hopkins Press, 1967.

King, Jr., Martin Luther. *Stride Toward Freedom.* New York: Harper and Brothers, 1958.

————. *The Measure of a Man.* Philadelphia: Christian Education Press, 1959.

————. *Strength to Love.* New York: Pocket Books, 1964.

————. *Why We Can't Wait.* New York: Harper and Row, 1964.

————. *A Martin Luther King Treasury.* New York: Educational Heritage, 1964.

————. *The Trumpet of Conscience.* New York: Harper and Row, 1967.

————. *Where Do We Go From Here: Chaos or Community?* New York: Harper and Row, 1967.

Kuper, Leo. *Passive Resistance in South Africa.* New Haven: Yale University Press, 1957.

Laski, H. J. *Authority in the Modern State.* New Haven: Yale University Press, 1919.

Legum, Colim, ed. *Pan-Africanism.* Ithaca: Cornell University Press, 1966.

Lewis, Anthony. *Portrait of the Decade.* New York: Bantam Books, 1965.

Litwack, Leon. *North of Slavery: The Negro in the Free States, 1790–1860.* Chicago: University of Chicago Press, 1961.

Logan, Rayford. *The Negro In the United States.* New York: The Macmillan Co., 1957.

Lubell, Samuel. *White and Black: Test of a Nation.* New York: Harper and Row, 1964.

Luthuli, Albert. *Let My People Go*. New York: McGraw-Hill, 1962.

Mayo, Henry B. *An Introduction to Democratic Theory*. New York: Oxford University Press, 1960.

McClellan, Grant, ed. *Civil Rights*. New York: H. W. Wilson, 1964.

McCoy, Charles. *The Structure of Political Thought*. New York: McGraw-Hill, 1963.

McIver, Robert. *The Modern State*. London: Oxford University Press, 1926.

Meier, August. *Negro Thought in America, 1880–1915*. Ann Arbor: University of Michigan Press, 1963.

Michele, Roberto. *Political Parties*. New York: Dover Publications, 1959.

Miller, W. R. *Non-Violence: A Christian Interpretation*. New York: Association Press, 1964.

Myrdal, Gunnar. *An American Dilemma*. New York: Harper and Row, 1942.

Newby, I. A. *The Development of Segregationist Thought*. Homewood, N.J.: Dorsey Press, 1968.

Niebuhr, Reinhold. *The Nature and Destiny of Man*. 2 vols. New York: Charles Scribner's Sons, 1949.

————. *Moral Man and Immoral Society*. New York: Charles Scribner's Sons, 1960.

Nowlin, W. *The Negro in American National Politics*. Boston: Stratford Co., 1924.

Peck, James. *Freedom Ride*. New York: Simon and Schuster, 1962.

Phillips, U. B. *American Negro Slavery*. New York: D. Appleton and Company, 1918.

Plamenatz, J. P. *Consent, Freedom and Political Obligation*. London: Oxford University Press, 1928.

Powell, Adam C. *Marching Blacks*. New York: Dial Press, 1945.

Preston, Edward. *Martin Luther King: Fighter For Freedom*. Garden City, N.J.: Doubleday and Co., 1969.

Rashdall, H. *The Theory of Good and Evil*. London: Oxford University Press, 1907.

Reddick, L. D. *Crusader Without Violence*. New York: Harper and Row, 1959.

Reuter, E. B. *The American Race Problem*. New York: Thomas Crowell Co., 1938.

Ross, W. D. *The Right and the Good*. Oxford: Clarendon Press, 1930.

Schlesinger, Arthur. *A Thousand Days*. New York: Houghton Mifflin, 1965.

Silversmith, Arthur. *The First Emancipation*. Chicago: University of Chicago Press, 1967.

Smith, T. V. *The American Philosophy of Equality*. Chicago: University of Chicago Press, 1927.

Sorel, George. *Reflections on Violence*. Trans. T. E. Hulme and J. Ruth. Glencoe, Ill.: Free Press, 1953.

Spitz, David. *Patterns of Anti-Democratic Thought*. New York: The Macmillan Co., 1949.

————. *Democracy and the Challenge of Power*. New York: Columbia University Press, 1958.

Strauss, Leo. *What Is Political Philosophy?* Glencoe, Ill.: Free Press, 1959.

Tannerbaum, Frank. *Slave and Citizen*. New York: Vintage Books, 1964.

Tawney, R. H. *Equality*. New York: Harcourt, Brace and World, 1931.

Thorpe, Earl E. *The Mind of the Negro: An Intellectual History of Afro-Americans*. Baton Rouge: Ortlieb Press, 1961.

Thurman, Howard. *Jesus and the Disinherited*. New York: Abingdon-Cokesbury Press, 1949.

Urquhart, W. S. *Pantheism and the Value of Life*. Oxford: The University Press, 1925.

Wagstaff, Thomas, ed. *Black Power*. Beverly Hills, California: Glencoe Press, 1969.

Wanlass, Lawrence. *Gettell's History of Political Thought*. New York: Appleton-Century-Crofts, 1951.

Washington, Jr., Joseph R. *Black Religion.* Boston: Beacon Press, 1964.

Weatherford, W. D. *The Negro From Africa to America.* New York: George Doran Co., 1924.

Westin, Alan R., ed. *Freedom Now.* New York: Basic Books, 1964.

Williams, G. W. *History of the Negro Race in America: 1619–1880.* New York: Putnam's Sons, 1915.

Wolin, Sheldon S. *Politics and Vision.* Boston: Little, Brown and Co., 1960.

Woodward, C. Vann. *Origins of the New South.* New York: Oxford University Press, 1951.

ARTICLES AND PERIODICALS

Braden, Anne. "The Southern Freedom Movement in Perspective," *Monthly Review* (July–August, 1965): 1–93.

Brossard, C. "A Cry From Harlem," *Look Magazine* 7 (December 14, 1965): 125–128.

Coser, Lewis A. "Some Social Functions of Violence," *The Annals* 371 (March 1966): 8–18.

Dickenson, John. "A Working Theory of Sovereignty," *Political Science Quarterly* (March 1928): 32–63.

Fleming, Walter. " 'Pap' Singleton, The Moses of the Colored Exodus," *American Journal of Sociology* 15.

Garvin, R. "Benjamin or 'Pap' Singleton and His Followers," *Journal of Negro History* (January 1948): 7–23.

Germino, Dante L. "Two Types of Recent Christian Political Thought," *Journal of Politics* 12 (August 1959): 455–486.

Hare, Nathan. "An Epitaph for Nonviolence," *Negro Digest* 3 (January 1966): 15–20.

King, Jr., Martin Luther. "We Are Still Walking," *Liberation* 5 (December 1956): 6–9.

————. "Our Struggle," *Liberation* 4 (April 1957): 1–4.

————. "Nonviolence and Racial Justice," *The Christian Century* 13 (February 6, 1957): 165–167.

————. "The Most Durable Power," *The Christian Century* 74 (June 5, 1957): 708–709.

————. "Facing the Challenge of a New Age," *Phylon* 10 (December 1957): 25–27.

————. "Pilgrimage to Nonviolence," *The Christian Century* 75 (April 13, 1960): 439–442.

————. "Suffering and Faith," *The Christian Century* 76 (April 27, 1969): 510.

————. "The Burning Truth in the South," *The Progressive* 12 (May 1960): 8–9.

————. "Equality Now," *The Nation* 192 (February 4, 1961): 91–95.

————. "The Time for Freedom Has Come," *The New York Times Magazine* (September 10, 1961): 3–6.

————. "Love, Law and Civil Disobedience," *New South* (December 1961): 3–11.

————. "Fumbling on the New Frontier," *The Nation* 194 (March 3, 1962): 190–193.

————. "The Case Against Tokenism," *The New York Times Magazine* (August 5, 1962): 2–4.

————. "Bold Design for a New South," *The Nation* 196 (March 30, 1963): 11–14.

————. "Letter From Birmingham Jail," *The Christian Century* 75 (June 12, 1963): 767–769.

————. "Letter From Birmingham Jail," *New South* (May 1963): 3–14.

————. "The Negro Is Your Brother," *Atlantic Monthly* 9 (August, 1963): 77–79.

————. "Hammer of Civil Rights," *The Nation* 200 (March 9, 1964): 185–191.

————. "Negroes Are Not Moving Too Fast," *Saturday Evening Post* 10 (November 7, 1964): 8–10.

————. "The Nobel Prize," *Liberation* 3 (January 1965): 28–29.

————. "Behind the Selma March," *Saturday Review* 16 (March 3, 1965): 16–17.

_____. "Let Justice Roll Down," *The Nation* 202 (March 15, 1965): 269–274.

_____. "The Un-Christian Christian," *Ebony* 16 (August 1965): 78–81.

_____. "Next Stop: The North," *Saturday Review* 8 (November 13, 1965): 33–35.

_____. "Nonviolence: The Only Road to Freedom," *Ebony Magazine* 20 (October 1966): 27–35.

Leonard, Edward A. "Ninety-Four Years of Non-Violence," *New South* 20 (April 1965): 4–7.

Loewenstein, Karl. "Political Systems, Ideologies and Institutions: The Problem of Their Circulation," *Western Political Quarterly* 18 (December 1953): 689–706.

Metha, Ved. "Gandhism Is Not Easily Copied," *New York Times Magazine* (July 9, 1961): 8–11.

Nieburg, H. L. "The Threat of Violence and Social Change," *American Political Science Review* 63 (December 1962), 865–873.

_____. "Uses of Violence," *Journal of Conflict Resolution* 8 (March 1963): 43–54.

Sharma, Mohan L. "Martin Luther King: Modern America's Greatest Theologian of Social Action," *Journal of Negro History* 53 (July 1968): 257–263.

Smith, Lillian. "A Strange Kind of Love," *Saturday Review* 20 (October 20, 1962): 18–20.

Spitz, David. "Democracy and the Problem of Civil Disobedience," *American Political Science Review* 24 (June 1954): 386–403.

Thorpe, Earl E. "The Central Theme of Negro History," *Carson–Newman College Faculty Studies Bulletin* 2 (April 1969): 13–19.

Walton, Jr., Hanes, "The Political Leadership of Martin Luther King, Jr.," *The Quarterly Review of Higher Education Among Negroes* 36 (July 1968): 163–171.

Zinn, Howard. "The Force of Non-Violence," *The Nation* 204 (March 17, 1962): 227–233.

————. "Setting the Moral Equation," *The Nation* 207 (January 17, 1966): 64–69.

"The Destruction of Negro Families," *Current* 6 (November 1965): 6–13.

UNPUBLISHED MATERIAL

King, Jr., Martin Luther. "A Comparison of the Conceptions of God in the Thinking of Paul Tillich and Henry Nelson Wieman." Ph.D. dissertation, Boston University, 1955.

Willingham, Alex. "The Religious Basis for Action in the Political Philosophy of Martin Luther King, Jr." M.A. thesis, University of Iowa, 1965.

Index

Abolitionists, xxiii
Africa, return to, 19, 21
African slaves, in colonial period, 12. *See also* slavery
agape: criticism of, 78; failure of, 79–80; God and, 79; as redemptive love, 65
aggressiveness, of young blacks, 25
alliances and coalitions, black power distrust of, 91–93, 113
American Creed, restriction of, xxxv
American Dream: Black Revolution and, xxxi; promise vs. performance in, xxxiv; racism and, xx, xxxiv
American life, tragic incongruities in, xxxiv
American Revolution: Black Revolution and, xxxii–xxxiii; social goals of, xxx
anti-Communism, 21
anti-Garveyism, 21
Aquinas, St. Thomas, 69
Aristotle, 42, 77, 114
armed forces, segregation in, 29
Atlanta, Ga., King's early years in, 41
Atlanta Cotton Exposition, 19
Augustine, St., 7, 67, 69

backlash, self-help and, 97
barbers, refusal of to serve Negroes, 27

beloved community, King's concept of, 8, 69–74
Bennett, Lerone, Jr., 95
Bentham, Jeremy, 42–43
Bill of Rights, U.S. Constitution, 8
"bill of rights for disadvantaged," 71–72
black college graduate, first, 13
black community: first task of, 92; King's assurance of nonviolence in, 104
black encounter: "meaningless" nature of, xix; in political science, xxv
black experience: American pretensions and, xxi; democratic ideals and, xviii–xix, xxxi; reality of, xxvii
black heaven, fantasy of, 22
black history, common core of, 18
black life, perversion of democracy and, xxiii
black man (black people): alienation of, xxv; alliances with labor organizations, 97, 113; alliances with white community, 91–93; attacks on discrimination by, 13–14; basic rights of, 7; Democratic party alignment in, 98; disenfranchisement of (1876), 18–19; early paths to freedom for, 10–36; "embracing of nonviolence by," 104; exclusion from World War II production boom, 26; first mass

129

xvii, xxiv; in colonial period,
12; vs. democracy, xxx; Greeks
and, xxiv; moralizing of, xxii;
national unity and, xxii; as
"necessary evil," xxii; as racism,
xvi
slaves: dehumanizing of, xxii; insurrection of in Charleston
(1822), 15; role of in American
political thought, xv
social contract, 7, 43
social Darwinism, racism and, 19
social justice, defined, 10–11
social philosophy, and nature of
man, 3
social progress, concept of, 61–62
social reform: love and, 45–46;
violence and, 110
social scientists, treatment of Negro by, xxiv
social values, in political thought,
4
society: human rights in, 4–5;
justice in, 11
Socrates, 5–6, 93
Sojourner Truth, 16
soul-saving, vs. self-respect, 25
South: education for blacks in,
14–15; school closings in, before
Civil War, 16; slave liberations
in, 14; slavery states before
Civil War, 14
Southern Christian Leadership
Conference, 30
Southern Negro, migration to
North of, 20. *See also* black
man; Negro
Southern political thought, xvi
Southern schools, 14–15
Spirit of '76, black people and,
xxxi
stable society, human rights and,
4–5
state: equated with God, 94; right
to punish lawbreakers, 95–96;
right to violence, 112
Strauss, Leo, 4
suffering: redemptive nature of,
58; willingness in, 69

"talented tenth," Du Bois on, 20
theology, defined, 114
Thoreau, Henry David, 41, 44, 94,
99
Thurman, Howard, 24, 29
Tobias, Channing, 24–25
Tocqueville, Alexis de, xvi, xxviii
Toomer, Jean, 31
Trotter, Monroe, 20
Truman, Harry S., 29
Tubman, Harriet, 16
Turner, H. M., 19
Turner, Nat, 15

underground railroad, 16–17
union leaders, in New Deal era,
23. *See also* labor unions
United States: "born free" meaning in, xxxii; democracy as
"given" in, xxix; moral ambiguity in, xxi; open or equalitarian society in, 10; political
thought and slave controversy
in, xv; self-image of, xix
Universal Negro Improvement
Association, 21
unjust law, 67
utilitarianism, 42–43

value judgments, experience and,
xxiv–xxv
Ved Metha, 87
Vesey, Denmark, 15
violence: as "American as cherry
pie," 90; coercion in, 85–86; defined, 82; forms of, 82–83; hate
and, 78; as immoral, 59–60;
King's views on, 82; vs. nonviolence, 91; relative values of, 110;
self-defeating nature of, 26;
states' right to, 112; threat of,
85; for worthy cause, 110
voting, majority power in, xviii

Walton, Hanes, Jr., xxxvii
war materials, production of, 23
Washington, Booker T., 19, 34,
73, 113
Washington, George, xxxiii